D1226955

CONTEMPORARY SOVIET
MILITARY AFFAIRS

CONTEMPORARY SOVIET MILITARY AFFAIRS

The Legacy of World War II

Edited by

JONATHAN R. ADELMAN
CRISTANN LEA GIBSON

Boston
UNWIN HYMAN
London   Sydney   Wellington

Unwin Hyman, Inc.
8 Winchester Place, Winchester, Mass. 01890, USA

Published by the Academic Division of
Unwin Hyman Ltd
15/17 Broadwick Street, London W1V 1FP, UK

Allen & Unwin (Australia) Ltd,
8 Napier Street, North Sydney, NSW 2060, Australia

Allen & Unwin (New Zealand) Ltd in association with the
Port Nicholson Press Ltd,
Compusales Building, 75 Ghuznee Street, Wellington 1, New Zealand

First published in 1989

Library of Congress Cataloging-in-Publication Data

Contemporary Soviet military affairs: the legacy of World War II
edited by Jonathan R. Adelman and Cristann Lea Gibson.
    p.   cm.
Bibliography: p.
Includes index.
ISBN 0-04-445031-1. — ISBN 0-04-445051-6 (pbk.)
1. Military art and science—Soviet Union—History—20th century.
2. World War, 1939–1945—Influence.   I. Adelman, Jonathan R.
II. Gibson, Cristann Lea.
U43.S65C66   1989   88-32731 CIP
355'.00947—dc19

British Library Cataloguing in Publication Data

Contemporary Soviet military affairs: the legacy of World War II
1. Soviet Union. Military power
I. Adelman, Jonathan R.   II. Gibson, Cristann Lea
355'.0332'47
ISBN 0-04-445031-1
ISBN 0-04-445051-6 (pbk.)

Typeset in 10/12 point Garamond by Fotographics (Bedford) Ltd
and printed in Great Britain by Billings and Son, London and Worcester

Contents

To Dora
my ineffable and incomparable bubbileh

To my parents
Dr. Ralph R. Gibson and Wanda Gibson

and to my husband
Dr. Stephen M. Meyer

1

Introduction

Jonathan R. Adelman

World War II was an event of great impact on the Soviet Union in general and the Red Army in particular. Western scholars have often echoed Seweryn Bialer when he wrote of the "four decisive war years" as an "experience (that) was undoubtedly crucial in forming what is today the political, economic, scientific, cultural and military elite in the Soviet Union" (1970: 14). Furthermore, scholars and analysts alike have frequently, if fleetingly, invoked the importance of the war for understanding the Soviet experience. For example, Soviet Chief of Staff Marshal Sergei Akhromeyev, on his recent tour of the United States in July 1988, stated that the two most important events in his life were the siege of Leningrad (in which he participated) and the signing of the International Nuclear Forces (INF) Treaty.[1] Hence the study of World War II becomes an integral and vital aspect in the study of the Soviet Union.

It is, therefore, remarkable that the study of the Soviet experience in the war has been largely neglected in the West. Until several years ago there was not a single major study of the Soviet economy or polity during the war, nor even any overall consideration of the impact of World War II on Soviet politics. Only in the military arena were there several strictly historical studies of the Red Army in the war (Clark 1965; Ziemke 1968; and Seaton 1970). In the last few years the situation has improved with the publication of a detailed two volume history of the Red Army in the war (Erickson 1975, 1983), an edited work looking at the impact of the war on the

Soviet Union (Linz 1985) and a detailed study of the Soviet wartime economy (Harrison 1985). Even with these gains the omission of a discussion of the military from the Linz volume and the lack of any consideration of the impact of the war on the future of the Soviet military in any of the battlefield histories of the Red Army illustrate the long distance that remains to be trod. For as James Millar has written,

> No society in modern time has absorbed a blow of the severity of Operation Barbarossa and survived as a political, economic and social entity. The Soviet experience in World War II and its impact upon postwar Soviet society have scarcely been charted by Western students of Soviet society. As a consequence, the war and immediate postwar periods are the least understood of the years since 1917. (Linz 1985: 283)

This neglect is doubly important since the lessons of the war for the Soviet Union and the United States were markedly different. Any attempt to simply transpose American experience and Soviet experience would be misleading. For the United States had an essentially "good war" while the Soviet Union underwent a national catastrophe. Stephen Cohen has described the gulf between the lessons drawn from their participation in the same war:

> For most of us in the West, World War II is a remote and half-forgotten historical event. For Soviet citizens, however, it is the "Great Patriotic War" and a traumatic experience that ended "only yesterday.". . . More than any other event, including the Russian Revolution, the war shaped the Soviet Union as it exists today, as a political system, society and world power. Its legacy endured among citizens because it was an experience of inseparable—and colossal—tragedy and triumph. (Cohen 1985: 1)

Perhaps now, as we move towards the fiftieth anniversaries of the major events of World War II, there is a good chance to reflect on the impact of the war on the Soviet Union. The war's impact reached its zenith during the Brezhnev era and is now inevitably in decline. A new postwar generation is coming to power under Gorbachev, who is concomitantly beginning to play down the war experience. This, then, is a good time to take stock of what were the ephemeral and what were the lasting impacts of the war on the Soviet military under vastly changed contemporary battlefield conditions.

It is important to add as well that this volume will not be looking at the entire postwar era (as interesting as that might be) but rather it will focus on the Soviet military at the end of the 1980s and on the war itself. Thus instead of looking at the evolution of views over time it will focus on the contemporary military and the war experience. There is no need to look at the military-technical dimension in the introduction since it is well covered throughout the book. Rather I will lay the groundwork for documenting the impact of the World War II experience on the Soviet psyche. This will allow us to look at the impact of World War II on different areas of military thought and action in the very different contemporary military environment. In the conclusion we will look at what aspects of the war experience are and are not relevant to contemporary Soviet military affairs.

The Nature of World War II

The Second World War was an event of great significance for the Soviet Union in particular and international politics in general. The war marked an historic change in the international system. For almost three hundred years, from the Treaty of Westphalia in 1648 until the start of World War II, international politics had been largely reducible to European politics. Within that system a loose balance of power revolving around six to eight predominantly European countries had prevailed, except for the intermittent interludes of the Napoleonic Wars. Despite significant and recurrent intrasystemic clashes, the European polity had been marked by relative cultural and often political homogeneity, which had facilitated the role of England as the balancer and maintainer of the system. Given conventional weapons and the shifting power relations, the differences among nations were relative, not absolute, and subject to frequent changes.

World War II changed all of this, smashing forever the Eurocentric balance of power system. In its place arose initially a tight, and then later a loose bipolar system revolving around two hitherto peripheral and non-Western European actors, the United States and the Soviet Union. The destruction of German and Japanese military power, coupled with the exhaustion of England and France, removed any serious competition for the two superpowers. As new and inexperienced powers with deeply antagonistic interests and perceptions, the superpowers were bound to create a new international system. With the advent of nuclear weapons, the new system was marked from its inception with a level of destructiveness and possible finality unheralded in international politics. At the same time, the possession of large arsenals of nuclear weapons would serve to make the gap between the two superpowers and the second-ranking powers absolute rather than relative. The ideological rivalry between American democratic capitalism and Russian authoritarian socialism would promote a new cold war and protracted hostilities between the two sides that were only an isolated feature of the previous system. And it would also foster a tight clash between the two camps in which neutrality or shifting of sides, once so prominent a feature of the preceding system, would become a rare, if almost nonexistent, event.

If World War II created the first new international system in three centuries, it also had a profound impact on Russia. For almost a century Russian military and political power had been in sharp decline. Recurrent defeats in the Crimean War, Russo-Japanese War and especially World War I had made the glories of Tsar Alexander's entrance into Paris in 1814 seem very distant indeed. The conclusion of the humiliating Treaty of Brest-Litovsk, which gained Russian withdrawal from the war at the price of enormous territorial sacrifice in 1918, symbolized the decline in Russia's power. The exclusion of Russia from the Munich Conference in 1938, the devastation wreaked by Stalin on the Red Army in the Great Purges, the poor performance in the Winter War with Finland, and the spurring of Russia's proferred hand for a military alliance with France and England seemed to indicate that the Bolsheviks had not reversed the secular decline in Russian power. The early massive reversals of the first two years of the Russo-German clash in World War II, in which the Germans occupied territory six times the size of Germany on which 85 million Russians had lived before the war, made any significant change in Russia's status seem unlikely.

It was against this black background of being the "sick man" of Europe for a century that the victories of 1943-45, and the emergence of the Soviet Union as a superpower after the war, appeared to be a miracle. In 1942 Stalin merely hoped to survive the German onslaught; in 1945 his soldiers would stand in Berlin,

Prague and Budapest, planning to divide Europe with the Americans and English. The destruction of the dreaded German and Japanese empires, and their permanent elimination as a threat to Moscow, coupled with Russia's rise to great power during the course of the war, made World War II truly historic for the Soviet Union; so, too, did the gaining of Eastern Europe as a "prize" from the war.

The sudden rise of the Soviet Union thereby coincided with the emergence of a new international system in which it played a powerful role. This alone would have been enough to make the war a powerful formative experience for the Soviet Union. But several other factors deeply reinforced this tendency. The most important one was the tremendous cost and sacrifice of the war, a cost that would be felt for decades to come.

The figures alone are numbing—20 million deaths, 30 million casualties, 25 million homeless, 10 million unborn children, millions left permanently maimed or crippled. Another 17 to 25 million people fled eastward in the path of the German advance in 1941 and 1942, leaving everything behind as they became impoverished refugees in their own country. Even during the war 1 to 2 million minority nationalities were deported, 22 million Eastern Europeans were annexed to the Soviet Union by 1945, and roughly 3 million people emigrated or remained abroad after the war. Over 5 million Russians returned to the Soviet Union after the war. The Soviet population of 1941 was not regained until 1956. By 1945 there were 20 million more women than men in the Soviet Union. By one Soviet calculation the 1959 population was 50 million people less than would have been expected without a war. The war reached into every household, killing, maiming, evacuating or leaving homeless perhaps 40 percent of the prewar Soviet population. And almost 35 percent of the Soviet population suffered through an average of two to three years of German occupation, which was designed to humiliate the Russian and non-Russian *untermenschen* (inferior people). The costs of the war touched every family, inflicting pain, suffering, and enormous mental or physical suffering on nearly everyone for close to four long years. Thanks to German barbarism, the usual line between soldiers and civilians vanished; battle losses and suffering were almost evenly divided between the two groups in many areas of western Russia (Linz 1985: 130–34, 207).

For the Soviet Union the war had an impact similar (but on a lesser relative scale) to the Holocaust for European Jewry, with which it overlapped. For the bulk of the Holocaust occurred not in Germany or Western Europe but in Poland, Russia, and the Baltics. The war in both cases was a tremendous event of world historical importance, casting doubt on the very existence of the state or the people. The mass slaughter and relentless German advance from 1939 through 1942 made mere survival for the Jewish people and the Soviet Union seem unlikely against the seemingly inexhaustible power of the Third Reich, which was determined to liquidate what it bizarrely termed the "Jewish-Bolshevik menace." How could the Soviet Union survive after the early disasters and loss of territory by late 1942, territory on which 40 percent of the population had lived before the war?

Yet, by the end of the war the Soviet Union emerged triumphant as a superpower with its enemies destroyed and occupied by the Allies, just as the majority of world Jewry survived and created the state of Israel (ironically, largely with the aid of Soviet-supplied weapons and socialist ideals). Neither group had expected great results early in the war, when mere survival seemed to signify a major victory. The great advances of the Red Army westward, coupled with Allied progress in the west, erased Nazi Germany and the permanent threat to Russian (and Jewish) survival.

A second important factor was that the Soviets had the perception that they had defeated Nazi Germany, the most powerful hegemonic and imperialist power in modern history, largely on their own efforts. This made the final victory seem all the more amazing. To Westerners, Soviet claims in this regard seem largely propagandistic, and, of course, to a certain degree they do deliberately exaggerate reality. But this easy dismissal of Soviet claims ignores the extent to which Russians genuinely believe that the victory *was* largely of their own making.

A look at the circumstances of the war can help explain this phenomenon. For over 1,000 days, from June 1941 until June 1944, the Russians fought desperate and enormously savage battles, from Moscow and Leningrad to Stalingrad and Kursk-Orel, on the Eastern front. The size and scope of these battles were unequalled in military history; in these titanic battles, the Red Army lost over 11 million men, killed or taken captive by the Germans. For this staggering cost they drove the Wehrmacht out of nearly all of Russia, save for Belorussia and the Baltics, while inflicting over

2 million permanent losses on the mauled German forces (Urlanis 1971; Jung 1971: 282, 289).

During this time it seemed to the Russians that the American and British forces were everywhere except where they should be—in France opening a strong second front against the Germans. The Anglo-American allies were securing the Atlantic Ocean, bombing Germany, invading the periphery of the Third Reich in North Africa, Sicily, and Italy and sending limited Lend Lease supplies to Russia. But while the Red Army was engaging perhaps 200 German divisions, the Allies were occupying only several dozen German divisions. And while the Red Army was losing 11 million men, the Allies had probably not even lost 200,000 men by D-Day (Adelman 1988). By the time the Allies did come in force to Europe at Normandy, the Russians felt that they had already largely won the war on their own efforts because the Germans were everywhere in defeat.

This image was strengthened by the last year of the war. Even at this time the Allies did not seem to be carrying their weight in the war. Rather they relied on the Red Army to absorb the bulk and fury of the remaining Wehrmacht power while they were content to save casualties and punish the Third Reich from afar through strategic bombing campaigns and safe ground advances against dwindling German forces. The Russian suspicions were aroused because the Germans kept roughly two-thirds of their land forces in the East (except for the Battle of the Bulge) and fought with far more savagery in the East than in the West. Especially after Normandy and the Battle of the Bulge there was nothing in the West to compare with the ferocity of the battle for East Prussia, the Hungarian campaign, or the siege and capture of Berlin in the east. The casualty statistics bear this out: 200,000 American and British battle fatalities compared to 1,200,000 Russian battle deaths in the final year of the war in Europe (Linz 1985: 1). All this simply fed the Russian feeling—especially when they were living in primitive conditions while the Americans, who were sheltered from the war, enjoyed an economic boom—that the Soviet Union had won the war with minimal and reluctant help from its western allies.

A third factor of considerable importance in projecting the war as a major formative experience in Soviet history was the history of the preceding almost quarter century since the October Revolution. The revolution and ensuing civil war had deeply divided the Soviet Union. With over 11 million deaths, predominantly civilian, in the civil war and subsequent mass emigration from Russia, the narrow Bolshevik victory by the end of 1920 had left Lenin ruling a prostrate and deeply divided country. This had necessitated a major retreat from socialism throughout the 1920s, in the form of the New Economic Program, which was designed to placate an alien population. For example, in the countryside, where the bulk of the population lived, old forms remained dominant and Bolshevik influence was minimal. The upsurge of the 1930s, with massive programs of industrialization, modernization and collectivization, while registering crucially important industrial and educational gains, had further profoundly alienated large parts of the population. The Russian nationalism, Great Purges, brutality of collectivization and dekulakization and the cult of Stalin's personality had all deeply estranged powerful segments of Soviet society. This would be reflected in the early days of the war in the greeting given by a large part of the population of the occupied territories to the German invaders and by the poor performance of the Red Army.

World War II, then, for the first time, provided a strong integrating and unifying experience for the Soviet people and their state. This was especially the case after the Germans made clear their intent to exterminate millions of Russians, destroy the Russian state, and ignore the legitimate grievances of tens of millions of disgruntled Soviet citizens. In this struggle all Soviet citizens could participate, most voluntarily, and Stalin and the Soviet state could finally achieve a bond with the people. The phrase used in battle, "For Stalin, for the Fatherland," became the slogan for this new Soviet patriotism.

The war, then, became a great test for the Soviet system. Economically, it validated the Soviet command economy that was introduced with enormous sacrifice in the 1930s. Politically, it validated the great suffering endured in the 1930s as the price to pay for elevating the Soviet Union to superpower status by 1945. The victory in 1945 cemented the new bonds and legitimacy of a unified nation and a powerful Soviet government that had not only survived but triumphed over the Third Reich. The war thereby unified the nation and healed the extremely powerful divisions in Soviet society that had been reflected in the enormous power of the secret police before the war. It healed the generational divisions and

muted many of the other profound antagonisms that had traditionally plagued Russia, because all could unite to expel and conquer
Nazi Germany in this life and death struggle.

In this context the Soviet obsession with World War II, while
fostered by the political leadership, reflects a deep and genuine
Russian obsession with the war. Soviet presses have spewed forth
15,000 volumes on the war while Soviet military journals still
regularly refight key battles and campaigns from World War II
(Cohen 1985). Foreign observers in Moscow have regularly
commented on the heroic Soviet war mythology and the ongoing
massive focus on the war in novels, memoirs and movies. In the
1960s Mohammed Heykal relates, Egyptian President Gamal
Abdel Nasser used to warn Third World leaders headed for
Moscow, "You must resign yourself to hearing over and over again
about the experience of your interlocutors in the 'Great Patriotic
War' " (Heykal 1978: 27). More recently Robert Bathurst has
cogently observed,

> To make the rear aware that it, too, is on the front line, enormous
> attention is given to keeping alive memories of the last war. The message
> for the current generation is that it has an obligation to prepare for the
> same sacrifice as was made by the old revolutionaries and the Soviet
> population in World War II. . . . In a manifestation of that war, a recent
> fashion is for brides to go directly from their wedding ceremony to leave
> flowers at the memorial to the war dead. An attempt is made throughout
> the USSR to raise children in the spirit of self-sacrifice. . . . Claude Lévi-
> Strauss would find this indicative of an atmosphere far more obsessed
> than the one he found on Martinique in 1941. (Leebaert 1981: 36)

Dimensions of the Soviet Role in World War II

Since we deal predominantly with the military in this book, it is
important to sketch the broader context of the war to place it in
proper perspective. In this section we will focus on three aspects of
the war and the postwar era in the Soviet Union: economy, society
and politics. The economic cost of the war, both during its course
and in its aftermath, was heavy and protracted. Of course, war can
be stimulative for the economy, as seen by the 70 percent real gain
in United States Gross National Product during the war.[2] But this
involved variables such as a large, absorbable, unemployed labor

force, shelter from the ravages of war, and security against any debilitating invasion. All of these factors promoted the American effort: none were applicable to the Soviet war economy, already strained to the limit by 1941 and then subjected to the massive shocks of invasion and evacuation.

Although Lend Lease, reparations, and the acquisition of new territories and technologies did soften the blow somewhat, the accumulated impact of the war on the Soviet economy was enormous. During the war the loss of massive territories to the Germans in 1941 and 1942 intensified the severe difficulties faced by the Soviet leadership in fighting the economically and militarily superior German foe. Simple statistics tell part of the story. During the war the Germans destroyed 25–30 percent of all Soviet fixed capital stock, and by 1945 Soviet national income was 20 percent below the prewar level. The entire industrial geography of the country was changed during the war as the economy shifted eastward with over 80 percent of the industrial enterprises of the Ukraine, Belorussia and western Russia put out of action by the Germans for the course of the war. The massive population losses and tremendous destruction meted out to such key cities as Stalingrad and Leningrad would inevitably retard development for many years after the war. The war would further aggravate already depressed rural conditions.[3]

The impact on the postwar development of the Soviet Union would be felt for many years to come, even if territory newly acquired after the war partially softened that impact. The direct material losses alone have been calculated at eight to ten years of earnings of the prewar labor force, or two five-year plans. If the huge population losses are taken into account, then the carryover war losses rise to 18–25 years earnings of the prewar labor force (Linz 1985: 25). Furthermore, the low productivity in the early postwar years undoubtedly reflected the problems of reconversion from military to civilian production. Susan Linz concluded in her edited volume on World War II and its aftermath,

World War II caused a severe setback in the growth of output in the USSR. The ground lost in terms of the growth rate was not recovered by 1953, nor even by 1961. In large part this stems from the reduction in Soviet population and labor force, not only of the losses immediately attributable to World War II but also from the reduction of the Soviet leadership's capacity to expand the labor force. (Linz 1985: 21)

The impact on Soviet society was equally profound. We have already seen the awesome population statistics that show the deep impact of the war on average Soviet citizens. Life became extraordinarily grim as the standard of living, already low in 1940, dropped roughly 40 percent in real terms during the war (*Statistical* 1957: 5). Food was scarce and rationed, and many people lived near the verge of starvation. In a besieged city such as Leningrad over 600,000 Soviet citizens, twice the number of American battle deaths in the war, died, largely of starvation. Perhaps nowhere was life worse, though, than in rural areas. There the mass mobilization of manpower, equipment, and horses, together with the German occupation of vital agricultural land, the scorched earth policy, and the pressing needs of the army and the cities created horrendous problems. By 1945 women constituted 76 percent of the agricultural work force (Artiunian 1969: 75). In Alec Nove's telling words,

> Bare statistics do not begin to show how hard life was for the Soviet peasantry. Mechanical aids of all kinds became scarce or non-existent. Horses were mobilized, manual labor predominated. In areas over which the war had raged, many villages were destroyed. People lived in holes in the ground, used cows for ploughing, even put themselves into harness and pulled a plough or harrow. Artiunian cites memoirs: "We had to haul the plough. Eight or ten women harnessed themselves and hauled. We used a wider harness than the horses . . . We hauled a big stock to which the plough was attached. Behind the plough we had another woman or young lad." (Linz 1985: 81)

Nor did victory bring any immediate relief to Soviet suffering. The famine of 1946 ensured no end to Soviet rationing until 1947 and serious hunger plagued many rural regions. Stalinist anti-peasant policies, such as maintaining heavy taxes on private plots, increasing compulsory delivery quotas, and keeping procurement prices very low protracted the recovery period. Even by 1953, after agricultural recovery was completed, Soviet agricultural productivity would remain below the level of 1913.

The political impact of the war was equally considerable. For the masses of Soviet citizens the war and its outcome legitimized the regime and unified the nation. In particular, it enshrined Stalin with an almost godlike aura of infallibility for having whipped the Soviet state on to victory and superpower status against such enormous odds. This was to strongly contribute to the petrification of the last

years of Stalin and the creation of an authentic national base for his
near deification in those troubling years.

In a highly centralized, one-party state, though, the more
profound impact came within the party. Far from being a monolith,
the party itself had already undergone repeated transformations
and changes in the quarter century before the onset of World War
I. The sudden transition from a small and illegal underground party
before the February Revolution to the far larger mass mobilizing
party of the October Revolution and civil war was only the first of
several such changes. This was followed by the abolition of
intraparty democracy and the widescale purge of the old Bolsheviks
and the creation of a newly Stalinized party after 1927. Then this
new party was ravaged by the widescale devastation of the Great
Purges of the late 1930s and the emergence of a new, "mature"
Stalinized party by 1941. Any utility of the older prewar and civil
war models was further destroyed not only by the Great Purges
but also by the disasters in the Winter War with Finland and the
enormous magnitude of the disasters of 1941 and 1942.

The extent to which these events thoroughly decimated the old
elite generation needs to be briefly mentioned. The scale of the
Great Purges was awesome in its almost complete extirpation of
the elite generation—except for Stalin and a few top associates—
who had been ruling the Soviet Union ever since the October
Revolution. The numbers tell the story: 56 percent of the delegates
to the Seventeenth Party Congress (ironically named the Congress
of Victors) were arrested and many others were victims of suicide
and abandonment of politics, 70 percent of the alternate and full
members of the Central Committee elected in 1934 were arrested
and shot, others were dismissed and a phenomenal 85 percent of
provincial first party secretaries were purged. Even the officer
corps was not spared, losing one-third of its members with
especially high rates of decimation in the elite ranks. By 1939 a
startling 80 percent of the new Central Committee elected that year
were newly appointed elite members (Bialer 1980: 86–87). The old
elite generation was smashed, its members and their values and
policy culture openly denounced and dragged through the mud at
the spectacular show trials. In short, the Great Purges replaced and
shuffled "the overwhelming majority of the Soviet elites in all
spheres of endeavor and can rightfully be considered as tantamount
to a political revolution. Large parts of the elites disappeared

forever and the remainder of the elites and large parts of the subelites began to advance to higher posts at a breathtaking pace" (Bialer 1980: 86).

It was in this context of fluidity and frequent major changes that World War II was to have such an impact. For the Great Purges were still winding up when the Germans struck. The new party had no chance to consolidate itself before the onset of the war. The leaders of the postpurge generation, lacking any real political mentors because of the liquidation of their elders, created their own administrative style and routines free from the usual constraints, except for broad guidelines from Stalin. The war, thereby, literally socialized a new generation of party leaders and fostered a new administrative style, one whose legitimacy and influence was greatly strengthened by the illegitimacy of previous role models, the success in wartime, and the youth and inexperience of the leaders.

Certain characteristics of the postpurge generation that rose to power in the wake of the Great Purges further promoted the impact that World War II, and especially the years 1943–45, had on their attitudes. Most importantly, the postpurge generation was overwhelmingly young and inexperienced for the roles in which they suddenly found themselves thrust by their very rapid advancement. Nikolai Voznesenskii was only 35 when he headed Gosplan, Andrei Zhdanov 38 when he headed the Leningrad party organization, Nikita Khrushchev 40 when he ran the Ukrainian party organization and Nikolai Bulganin 42 when he was appointed chairman of the Russian Council of People's Commissars. This pattern was even more prominent at lower levels where Leonid Brezhnev and Mikhail Suslov were 33 and 37 years old, respectively, when they ran large Russian provinces, Alexei Kosygin was 35 when he became Deputy Prime Minister of the Soviet Union, and Dmitrii Ustinov was but 33 when he became People's Commissar of Armaments. Overall, by 1940 the Russian government was the youngest in modern history. In 1939 the average age of full members of the Central Committee was 44, of alternate members 37. This extreme youth of the elite made them impressionable, relatively free from past habits, extremely grateful to Stalin, and open to development of a new policy culture (Bialer 1980: 89). This also ensured their potential longevity in politics, which would last for four decades into the 1980s.

This susceptibility to new values and cultures was reinforced not only by their youth but also by their class background, education, and career experience. While the old elite had come from the urban intelligentsia and middle classes and often had a broad education and a lengthy history of political activism before 1917, the new elite was very different. Overwhelmingly it sprang from the working class and mainly the peasantry, reared thereby largely in small towns and villages remote from the main centers of power and culture. Many, if not most, actually engaged in physical labor while they were young. Their educational background was primarily technical and they became political generalists whose early advancement tended to be in the provinces. All of these traits accentuated their openness to the creation of a new policy culture divorced from the disgraced older one shared by leaders from different class and educational background and experiences. These relatively young and inexperienced men from the provinces with only narrow educational background would naturally look for a new modus operandi when they were suddenly granted enormous, undreamed of power by Stalin. They had only vague general guidelines, such as a natural passion for Stalin and the guiding line of Russian nationalism and socialism.

This is the final key point. Postpurgers came to power with incredible rapidity, without any preparation. Many, if not most, of those suddenly thrust into power failed and were dismissed. But those who succeeded were destined to rule Russia for several decades. The rise to power was storybook. Alexei Kosygin, from little-known factory director to Deputy Prime Minister in three years, Leonid Brezhnev from minor engineer in a factory to boss of a major industrial province in two and a half years. The consequences of this were awesome, even for those few who survived and went on to fame. For, as Seweryn Bialer has written,

In all cases the wholesale turnover of senior executive personnel left the administrative structure a shambles. The new executives, without experience to prepare themselves for the scope and burden of their new tasks, had to train on the job at the same time as they bore full responsibility for the every day task of government. The atmosphere of overwhelming fear generated by the Purges, the knowledge of what repercussions followed from a single misstep resulted in a situation where decision-making in Soviet state institutions—on the highest level as well as in trivial matters—tended to gravitate toward the ultimate center of power—Stalin. (1970: 89)

It was within this context, then, that World War II helped create and form the new elite generation in Soviet politics and shaped their values and sources of authority. Although the very top elite—Stalin and his associates in the Politburo (such as Lazar Kaganovich, Vyacheslav Molotov, Georgii Malenkov, Lavrentii Beria and Nikolai Voznesenskii)—did not change greatly in this period, they provided only general guidance for the new elite. When the war broke out, 70 percent of the people's commissars had been at their job for less than one year (Nekrich 1965). The intense four-year war experience, with all of the trauma of mass barbarism, repeated defeats, and near extinction leading eventually to great yet draining victories and the final attainment of victory and nascent super-power status, left its indelible mark on this generation. Only during the war was there finally elite stability and the creation of a strong bureaucratic war effort that allowed the emergence of a new policy culture. The new culture was formed by the nascent elite generation from the lower classes who saw in that culture the inevitable outcome and cause of the great triumphs of the Soviet Union in World War II.

This emerging postpurge generation would leave its impact on Soviet politics until the mid-1980s when it finally faded from the scene due to natural causes. As late as 1980 fully eleven of the fourteen full members of the Politburo and eleven of the fourteen members of the Presidium of the Council of Ministers belonged to the postpurge generation. In addition, one further member of the Politburo and two members of the Presidium joined the party during the war. Even at the lower level of department heads of the Central Committee Secretariat and members of the Council of Ministers roughly 60 percent were postpurgers and another 20 percent had joined during the war (Bialer 1980: 168). During the 1970s the postpurge elite maintained its grip on power by replacing members who died in office, such as Alexei Kosygin, Andrei Grechko, and Nikolai Shvernik, by others members of this generation, in this case Nikolai Tikhonov, Dmitrii Ustinov, and Arvid Pelshe. But this could not last forever and the deaths of such stalwarts as Leonid Brezhnev, Mikhail Suslov, Dmitrii Ustinov, Arvid Pelshe—and their immediate successors, such as Konstantin

Chernenko and Yuri Andropov—soon led to a massive generation turnover in the elite, only the second major change in the seventy-year history of the country.

The change was, of course, symbolized by the ascension to party leadership of Mikhail Gorbachev, who joined the party only in 1952. Clearly, the old elite is gone, as symbolized by the fact that in 1987 only two of the eleven full members of the Politburo. (Andrei Gromyko and Mikhail Solomentsev) had joined the party before the war as compared to five who joined after the war, from 1946 to 1957. The largest single group (four) joined during the war.

This does not mean, however, that the war experience has totally lost its meaning simply because the top leaders were not instrumental in fighting it. All of the top leaders remember it well, as they were 16–36 years old by its end. Many suffered directly from the war. Gorbachev's area in Stavropol was occupied by the Germans for six months and for several other months it was in or near the front. As a youth, then in his teens, he worked in the fields during the traumatic shortages and hard times induced by the war. Zdenek Mylnar, who knew Gorbachev from his time in Moscow, later wrote that the war, with its massive suffering, was a "fundamental experience for him" (Mylnar 1980: 27). Four of the top leaders (Ligachev, Solomentsev, Vorotnikov and Zaikov) worked in industrial plants during the war and two others (Chebrikov and Shcherbitsky) spent the war years in the Red Army. Only the younger generation of men, such as Gorbachev, Ryzhkov, and Shevardnadze, had no actual role in the war as they were still in school. Thus, the war had a profound impact on the postpurge generation and a residual impact on the current leaders of the Soviet Union.

The Military Dimension

It is against this backdrop of the dramatic impact of World War II on the civilian elite, which came to power in the aftermath of the Great Purges and dominated the postwar era until the rise of Gorbachev, that we can best understand the military elite. For the great impact of the war on civilian and military elites linked and fused them in a fundamental bond in the postwar years. The civilian political commissars and representatives in the army, such as

Khrushchev, Brezhnev, and Kirilenko, would retain their army connections in the postwar era and utilize them in the political sphere. Always there would be the intense emotional bond of a shared comradeship in the dire circumstances of war.

For the military elite the impact of the war was, naturally, even greater than on the civilian elite. The military, as a total institution with a strict code of honor, discipline, pride, and loyalty, had been deeply humiliated and cut to the quick by the Great Purges. The purge hit in direct proportion to the number of men holding a given rank, almost totally removing the great bulk of the military elite and leaving a deep stain on the military sense of honor. The numbers of those purged were overwhelming as shown below:

3 out of 5 marshals
15 out of 16 commanders, first and second rank
60 out of 67 corps commanders
126 out of 199 division commanders
221 out of 397 brigade commanders
1 out of 1 head of Main Political Administration
11 out of 11 deputy commanders of defense
1 out of 1 people's commisar of navy (Medvedev 1979: 192 ff.)

Suddenly, most of the top leaders, and nearly all of the creative and inspirational leaders of the Red Army—men such as Mikhail Tukhachevskii, Iona Yakir, Vasili Blyukher, Iyeronim Uborevich, Vitov Putna and Vitaly Primakov—were gone and disgraced as traitors and enemies of the people. The well-integrated army structure was shattered from the top down; the creative men who had followed changes in modern warfare and had been prepared to implement needed alterations in course were totally removed. As John Erickson has written about the Great Purges,

The list of the doomed men, distinguished and undistinguished alike, lengthened as the military purge gathered its dreadful momentum. The highest command echelons were hit hardest and longest. . . . In operational units there was, to use a Soviet euphemism, "severe shortage" of trained commanders. The military purge, which remains even now a goad to the Red Army's sense of its own honor, was not a short-lived spasm, but a political process, years in its duration, of basic if perverse importance to Stalin's rule in Stalin's fashion. The killings continued, the threat and then the actual advent of war notwithstanding, even into 1941. (Erickson 1975: 6)

The void was deep and profound and the protracted nature of the purges, which lasted right up and in some cases (Shtern and Smushkevich and the shooting of Western front officers) until after the beginning of the war, prevented any consolidation of a new culture. The deep fear and terror that permeated the Red Army even in the early months after the start of the war and the massive defeats of the first eighteen months further prevented any emergence of a new policy culture. So, too, did the very weak experience and education of the rising military elite of 1941. According to Soviet data in June 1941 only 7 percent of all officers had completed higher military education, 37 percent of the officers had not completed intermediate military education and a stunning 75 percent of all commanders had been in their positions for less than one year (Valenta and Potter 1984:7). Thus, the new army organization was inchoate at best, and would soon be further decimated by massive early wartime defeats.

A small group of Stalinist "Horse Marshals" ruled from 1937 until 1942. Men of limited horizon and civil war heroic vision, such as Semen Budenny, Kliment Voroshilov, and Semen Timoshenko, came to the fore. For these men of constrained imagination the problems of modern mobile warfare and the coordinated use of infantry, artillery, tanks, and planes—problems that had pre-occupied their purged predecessors—were simply of no great interest. Completely intellectually neutered, their main interests were total loyalty to Stalin, who had delivered them from the Great Purges and rewarded them with rapid advancement to positions for which they were not fit, and a dedication to replaying their civil war roles of romantic cavalry charges and men over machines. Their inadequacy was dramatically demonstrated in 1941 and 1942 when they were forced off the stage. The civil war model was discarded after the first years of the war in light of its irrelevance to modern warfare.

A new, and ultimately effective, military organization and culture literally formed on the battlefield in the midst of battle. The new policy culture emerged only after the elimination of the failed Stalinist commanders in 1941 and 1942, thus delaying the effective creation of a new leadership and policy culture until the period of 1943–45, the period that coincided with the great victories of World War II. It developed only against the backdrop of the extreme humiliation of the massive defeats of 1941 and 1942, thereby all the more highlighting their successes. The victory of this new elite generation and its policy culture against seemingly insuperable odds, and with evidently minimal Allied participation in that victory, endowed it with a sense of heroic and magnificent proportions. To the Red Army commanders victory seemed largely attributable to their own efforts. This wartime policy culture represented the flowering of a new professionalism in the army, of a proper balancing of armaments, equipment, and doctrine, of a new flexible responsiveness to the battlefield.

This rising elite generation in the military shared most of the same characteristics as its companion in the civilian sector. Overwhelmingly the new leaders were of working class and especially peasant background. Their educational background was narrow and technical, within the military sphere. Their rise to power came suddenly and at a very young and impressionable age. They came from obscurity and were totally loyal to the system and to Stalin. By the end of World War II they already formed a cohesive and strong new elite, powerful and self-confident, yet subordinate to Stalin.

If we look briefly at our sample of 33 top military commanders in 1947, the outlines of this generation become even more clear. By then all of the most famous commanders of World War II, such as Georgii Zhukov (although he was demoted), Ivan Konev, Aleksander Vasilevsky, Konstantin Rokossovsky and Ivan Bagramyan, were also the top leaders in the Soviet army in peacetime. They were relatively young—over 80 percent of them (27) were only in their forties or younger by the time the war ended in 1945. Over 80 percent of those on whom data is available came from the working class or, more often, the peasantry. And they were predominantly Russian (88 percent). Thus, in all essential features they matched the civilian elite.

Their professionalism was undoubted because slightly over half (17) were officers or noncommissioned officers in the Tsarist army of World War I. Then fully 90 percent (30) fought in the civil war, largely at the lower levels. A slight majority (16 of 30) on whom data is available joined the party during those trying days. Then during the interwar period, and especially during the 1930s, they gained the technical education they needed to function effectively in the military academies. Almost half (14) went to the elite Frunze Military Academy or the General Staff Academy. Thus, unlike the civilian elite, the rising military elite generally had strong technical skills (honed in the academies), practical military experience gained in World War I and the Russian Civil War, and a quarter century of military service before they suddenly rose to the top positions early in the world war.[4]

This military elite predominated until the 1970s when nature took its course. In its place came a new military elite consisting of leaders who had occupied lesser roles in the war. A sample of 21 top military commanders in 1987 shows this occurrence. No less than 90 percent of the military commanders (19) were then in their sixties and 90 percent had fought in the war. They were soldiers and low-ranking officers in the war. Fully 80 percent (16) joined the Red Army in the period 1937–41 before the war. Dmitrii Yazov, the new Defense Minister, has a typical biography. He was born in 1917, joined the Red Army in 1941, spent the war at the front, and entered the Communist party in 1944. No less than two-thirds (14) joined the party during the war.[5]

The significance of this is clear. Even over four decades after the end of the war, and with the passing of the postpurge military elite, the Soviet army still has many top commanders who are veterans of World War II. This war was the great formative experience of their youth. Perhaps because they saw it from the bottom rather than from the top, and because they were even younger at the time than the preceding generation, it undoubtedly has left a serious and lasting impression. In 1965 Alan Clark noted that the entire military elite was then dominated by heroes of the war, leading us to the need to remember the Soviet experience of World War II "and the extent to which it colors the hidden mainstream of Soviet strategy and memories of it which are born by every senior Soviet administrator, both military and civilian, at the present time" (Clark 1965: 465). This still remains true today, even if the torch has been passed to the soldiers and junior officers of that conflict.

Clearly, given the inevitable passing of time, this generation will pass from the scene within five to ten years, possibly less. And at the lower and middle levels of command this process has already occurred. The question then will become how enduring the war legacy, which impacted the Soviet army for half a century after its conclusion, will be for the succeeding generations that knew only of the war through books and tales.

The world has turned over many times since the historic events of World War II thrust the Soviet Union from the near oblivion of 1941 and 1942 to the great triumphs of 1945 and the attainment of superpower status. Yet, through these decades the enormous trauma of that war, the great sacrifices and the surprising victories, have remained the dominant formative experience for the military elite. They touched every Soviet officer personally, from the early ignominious defeats and retreats eastward to the redemption of the period of 1943–45. None have ever forgotten the grueling period that lasted almost four years and created a new Red Army and a new place for the Soviet Union in the world order. For each of them the war, while bringing personal tragedies and sorrows, also brought the great exhilaration of enormous, even breathtaking ascent to the very top of their profession and all the benefits that accrued therewith. It is little wonder that this victory has remained at the heart of the Soviet military experience, both collectively and individually, until the Gorbachev era. Only now, as we move into the era of *novaya myshlenie, glasnost* and *perestroika* has the World War II generation begun its inevitable fade from the scene and its influence has begun to decline concomitantly. But for over four decades it has remained a powerful influence on the Soviet military, one which will have an enduring impact even as the Soviet Union moves into the twenty-first century.

Notes

1 See *New York Times*, circa July 15, 1988.
2 For data on the United States war economy, see *Statistical* 1965: 139, 142, 178, 414.
3 For the best analysis of the Soviet war economy, see Harrison 1985.
4 For the 1947 sample see *Who* 1972.
5 For the 1987 sample see *Who's* 1984.

Part I

Relevance of History

2

Military History and the Experience of the Great Patriotic War

Eugene B. Rumer

In recent years Soviet military periodicals have turned their attention to the problems of Soviet military history and the shortcomings in the work of military historians. Perhaps, taking advantage of the general relaxation of the political atmosphere inside the Soviet Union and the reassessment of the state of affairs in virtually every sphere of the nation's life, including the defense sector, these journals have published many materials highly critical of the state of military-historical research in the USSR (Zhilin 1987: 56–61; Editorial 1987: 3–12).

Military historians were accused of failing to reach the level of competence necessary to deal with the problems facing Soviet armed forces today. The most important task facing them now is to meet the current practical demands of the armed forces. Military-historical research should be driven by concrete problems of military science. Today these include: mobilization and combat readiness; transition from peacetime to wartime posture; strategic deployment of the armed forces in world and local wars; beginning operations of the war; creation and use of strategic reserves.[1]

A sure sign of high-level concerns about the state of military-historical research was a conference that took place in the summer of 1987, sponsored by the Ministry of Defense and attended by leading military authorities. The purpose of this meeting was to assess the progress of military-historical science in the Soviet Union and chart new directions for research. The charges against military historians were the same: they have failed to meet the requirements generated by the current agenda of the armed forces.[2]

This preoccupation with the state of military-historical research in the Soviet Union should not be seen as a surprise or a new phenomenon. Rather, its emergence reflects the continuing importance of military history, in particular the experience of the Great Patriotic War and the impact it has had on the postwar development of Soviet military thinking. Practical applications of the results of military-historical research have long been a characteristic feature of Soviet military science and the experience of the Great Patriotic War has been among the key factors that have influenced postwar developments in Soviet military thinking.

In fact, as will be argued below, military history has been a discipline of great practical importance for the development of the Soviet armed forces throughout the entire postwar period. It is of much more than just academic or historical value for the Soviet military establishment and, therefore, could provide a number of useful insights for Western scholars of the Soviet Union and Soviet defense policy. This chapter is intended to demonstrate that in addition to the role assigned to military history in Soviet propaganda efforts, which will not be examined here, Soviet military history serves three functions: the objective historical; the scientific-pedagogical, and as a medium for surrogate discussions of current policy issues.[3]

The Three Functions of Military History

A telling example of the uses of military history in the USSR was a recent article published in the August 1987 issue of the leading Soviet journal *World Economy and International Affairs*. It was co-authored by a prominent civilian scholar of international relations Andrey Kokoshin and a distinguished military theorist Major General Vladimir Larionov (1987: 32–40). In an attempt to articulate a new strategic concept, they offered a radical revision of the experience of a key—the Kursk—battle of the Great Patriotic War.[4]

The article authored by Kokoshin and Larionov relied on the experience of a strategic defensive engagement of the Soviet army at Kursk to support an argument for defense as a viable strategy in a future war. Thus, the lead attack on Soviet strategic thought, which had relied on wartime experience to justify its offensive bias, was based on the assumption that the past war could offer many relevant lessons. Rather than challenging historical arguments as irrelevant in modern conditions, Kokoshin and Larionov put forth a revisionist interpretation of the Kursk battle. Like their opponents, the two advocates of strategic defense based their argument on the assumption that wartime experience matters.

This episode illustrates the meaning of the objective historical function. Historical experience is a major factor in the shaping of policy. This is true for any country and the Soviet Union is no exception to this general rule. Proponents of both offensive and defensive strategy are likely to look back at historical experience to support their arguments.

Soviet experience in World War II is particularly instructive with respect to potential military and political scenarios that might face Soviet leaders in the future. It would be naive to claim that history is likely to repeat itself precisely with respect to the potential missions facing the Soviet armed forces today. Such contingencies, however, have their origins in the war and a good deal in common with the Soviet army's missions of that period. The major strategic contingency facing the Soviet armed forces in the Eurasian continent remains the prospect that a two-front coalition war will be waged in similar geographic theaters against some of the same opponents who faced the Soviet Union in World War II. Indeed, under these circumstances history offers instructive lessons of immediate practical utility.[5]

Throughout the entire postwar period at every stage of the evolution of Soviet military doctrine the Great Patriotic War has remained the only concrete experience to which Soviet military experts could turn in search of practical answers to the issues facing them. No other source could rival it in terms of richness, breadth, and relevance of experience at every level of Soviet military art. Strategic lessons learned in the war covered such issues as the beginning period of war; mobilization and relocation of industry; strategic reserves; command and control. The war was the Soviet army's only encounter with modern operations involving tanks and mechanized troops. The theoretical foundations of Soviet operational art—the theory of deep operation—were developed in the 1930s. Their essence has not changed significantly since then, but the Great Patriotic War was the only real test of this theory. Similarly, at the tactical level the war remained a unique source of combat information, notwithstanding the progress of time and technology.

The study of the experience of the Great Patriotic War took place within the context of the prevailing doctrinal condition of a given moment. The focus of Soviet military scholars shifted as these conditions changed in order to highlight the aspects of wartime experience that were particularly relevant from the point of view of the current doctrine. In the immediate postwar period it was the tactical and operational experience of the war that drew the attention of Soviet military scholars interested in its practical application in the preparation and training of the armed forces. The development of nuclear weapons and the resulting doctrinal change refocused the Soviet military's attention on the strategic experience of the war, issues of prewar mobilization, war initiation, and surprise attack. Subsequent evolution of doctrine toward a more conventional posture highlighted once again the continuing relevance of the operational and tactical experience of the Great Patriotic War as well as its strategic lessons. The legacy of the Great Patriotic War and the evolution of military scholars' interest in its experience is reflected throughout Soviet military literature.

As was mentioned earlier, the objective historical function is not peculiar to the environment in which the development of Soviet military doctrine and military thought takes place, although due to the political and geographic factors it is, perhaps, more pronounced in the Soviet case. The other two functions of Soviet military-historical discipline—scientific-pedagogical and the medium for surrogate discussion of current policy issues—combined with the objective historical function, have given the objective historical function distinctly Soviet features.

Both these functions of Soviet military history are to a large extent derived from the continuing relevance of the historical experience to the issues facing the armed forces today. The Great Patriotic War offers rich and relevant material that can be used to educate new generations of officers and enlisted personnel about some of the likely contingencies that may face them in the future, as well as to guard them against committing the mistakes of the past.

Judging by Soviet military historians' near exclusive pre-occupation with various aspects of the Great Patriotic War, no other subject is currently or has been for a long time of greater relevance and utility for the development of Soviet military policy, doctrine, and the armed forces. No Soviet military author would deny the practical orientation of military history and in particular its utility from the point of view of military science, the education of new generations of officers, and day-to-day troop training. Military history is seen as the meeting point of two disciplines— military science and general history. The subject, goals and methods of military history are to a large extent defined by its two parent disciplines (Login 1979: 13–16).

The relationship between military science and military history in the USSR deserves a closer look for it explains the continuing influence of military history on research and the educational and training process in Soviet military academic establishments. Soviet military writers see the purpose of military science as the study of modern warfare intended to develop more effective methods of war fighting for today and tomorrow. As described in the 1986 edition of Soviet *Military Encyclopedic Dictionary* (*Voenny entsiklopedicheskii slovar'*), the main subject of military science is "armed struggle in wartime." Its purpose is to provide a sound basis for the development of military policy and doctrine.[6] Military science focuses primarily on current or recent matters, as they are the most relevant to its task (Login 1979: 13–16).

By comparison, military history, as a discipline with deep roots in general history, is broader in its scope because it deals with the history of war as a social phenomenon (Login 1979: 15–16). Its agenda, however, is driven by the practical considerations of Soviet military development, or, in the words of one Soviet military author, by the "needs of the epoch and the prevalent philosophical, political and military-doctrinal ideas" (Login 1979: 31–32). The degree of current relevance is the main criterion for choosing topics of military-historical research. Current relevance in turn is determined by the needs of military science, troop training, and the overall strengthening of the defense potential of the country (Login 1979: 31–32).

For example, Kokoshin and Larionov's interest in strategic defense at Kursk could be traced directly to recent efforts to formulate a new military doctrine based, presumably, on the principle of reasonable sufficiency or sufficiency for defense. The doctrinal shift set the guidelines for research of both military science and military history.

This does not mean that the experience of the Great Patriotic War offers ready recipes for the present or future. Soviet military writers are careful to add that much has changed since the end of the Great Patriotic War and that many of the principles derived from its experience require substantial corrections. But, they maintain, the main principles of Soviet military art and military leadership have retained their validity (Zhilin 1984: 359–360; Shavrov and Galkin 1977: 356).

This perspective on military history, and in particular the history of the Great Patriotic War from the point of view of military science, also makes it uniquely valuable for officer education and troop training, and, as will be demonstrated below, gives military history a special place on the curriculum of military institutions of higher learning.

While they are quick to praise military history for its contribution to military science and education of the officer corps, few Soviet military authors are likely to admit this discipline's function as a medium for surrogate debates of current policy issues. Yet it plays a very important role here.

Once again, Kokoshin and Larionov's article provided an excellent illustration of the uses of military history in the USSR. The currency of their analysis of the Kursk battle was highly transparent. It contained direct references to contemporary Soviet strategic thinking. Yet Kokoshin and Larionov chose to masquerade their challenge to current military thought as a historical revision. This choice provided them with an excuse, albeit a flimsy and obvious one, to protect themselves against the charges of indiscretion they might face for taking a sensitive doctrinal and strategic debate into the public arena.

Whereas an openly expressed opinion on matters of current defense policy may reveal too much to an unfriendly eye, a view couched in historical terms and backed by historical examples is likely to be less noticed by an outside observer and will certainly be more difficult to decipher. It will, however, reach the target audience whose ears are well attuned to the peculiarities of the message.

Another and less obvious example of such use of historical

experience is apparent in an earlier article by former Chief of the General Staff Marshal M. Zakharov. He argued before the leadership that they could not neglect the needs of the military on the eve of the Twenty-fourth Party Congress in 1971. Zakharov described how the Communist party assigned top priority to the needs of the defense sector in the course of the prewar five-year plans and praised the wisdom of this approach. The article was definitely not meant to be a historical overview, but an advocacy piece intended to remind the leaders to follow the positive example of their predecessors (Zakharov 1971: 3–12).

One obvious solution to the task of ensuring the secrecy of sensitive information would be to classify all military writings. This measure, however, would interfere with the training of soldiers and many lower- and mid-level officers. It would also require a substantial investment of resources in guarding this information. The alternative—setting the discussion in historical terms—helps avoid the complications associated with secrecy and at the same time provides a relatively safe medium.

The military-historical setting is appropriate for discussing current issues not only because it is "safe," but because of the impact the experience of the Great Patriotic War has had on the mind-set of the Soviet military establishment. For generations of Soviet officers the experience of the Great Patriotic War has been one of the most closely studied subjects in their professional education. Many war veterans and graduates of early postwar years are still on the faculties of military academies. For them the war was the major formative event of their professional careers. When faced with contemporary problems, they turn to the experience of the past war in search of a clue to the solution. In this sense, wartime experience has offered more than just a safe medium for potentially sensitive discussions; it has provided a virtually limitless pool of experience that could be helpful in dealing with many current issues.[7] Senior officers in turn have passed this approach on to their students through training and teaching. The war has had a lasting effect on the outlook of the wartime and immediate postwar generation of the Soviet military establishment, particularly on the education and thinking of the Soviet officer corps. Thus, the history of the Great Patriotic War has served as a medium for discussions of current policy issues and is both a discreet setting and a language in which the Soviet military establishment is fluent.

Military History at the General Staff Academy

An excellent illustration of the continuing importance of military history and in particular the history of the Great Patriotic War is offered in the two editions of the history of the Voroshilov General Staff Academy entitled *Akademiya general'nogo shtaba* and published in 1976 and 1987 (Kulikov 1976; Kozlov 1987). These books provide a good demonstration of the three functions of military history in the Soviet Union—objective historical, a medium for current policy discussions, and scientific-pedagogical.

The main item on the postwar agenda before the academy was the training of officers for the operational-strategic echelon (corps and above). Students were recruited from the ranks of senior officers and generals with operational command or staff experience during the war and prior degrees from their respective service academies (Kozlov 1987: 92). The curriculum placed heavy emphasis on the experience of the Great Patriotic War. Army- and front-level operations of the war constituted the primary case-study material from which the academy's students were supposed to learn operational and strategic wisdom (Kozlov 1987: 92). The department of strategy was established in 1946 with the specific mandate to study the strategic experience of the war. Strategy had not been taught at the academy prior to that point (Kozlov 1987: 98). Thus, the inauguration of the discipline occurred specifically in the context of wartime experience. The demand for military historians and teachers of the history of the war led to the establishment of a separate military-historical faculty within the academy in 1949 (Kulikov 1976: 117). As a result of the combat experience of the instructors and the historical nature of the curriculum, the study of the Great Patriotic War dominated every aspect of the teaching and learning process of the academy.

The year 1954 marked the beginning of a new stage in the work of the academy. The main task facing its faculty and students now was the study of operations involving the use of nuclear weapons (Kozlov 1987: 111, 113). In order to adapt to this new form of operations the academy was reorganized. Substantial changes were introduced in the curriculum of the academy. The first victim of the reorganization was the separate military-historical faculty, which had been disbanded even before the formal announcement of changes in the academy (Kozlov 1987: 113). By the late 1950s a unified program of instruction was adopted for students from all branches of the armed forces. Its main goal was to enhance the students' mastery of nuclear weapons and their operational-strategic use (Kozlov 1987: 114). The development of nuclear weapons had a major impact on the instruction in the history of wars and military art at the academy. The course now focused on the wartime experience of tank and mechanized troops, artillery, and the air force (Kozlov 1987: 116).

A major event in the history of the General Staff Academy, as well as a major turning point in Soviet postwar military development, was a lecture given at the academy by Chief of the General Staff Marshal Sokolovskii in August 1959 (Kulikov 1976: 152–53; Kozlov 1987: 119–20). The ideas expressed in Sokolovskii's lecture necessitated major revisions in the academy's curriculum, in particular in the course on strategy (Kulikov 1976: 152–53). An entirely new teaching program based on what the authors of the General Staff Academy history called a "new theoretical foundation" was introduced. The new curriculum focused on issues of war fighting in the conditions of early massed use of nuclear weapons and highly maneuverable operations of ground troops also involving the nuclear strikes (Kulikov 1976: 153, 160–61). Strategic goals in a future conflict would be accomplished by the Strategic Rocket Forces in cooperation with other services. The newly created branch of the Soviet armed forces—Strategic Rocket Forces—was capable of affecting the outcome of the beginning period as well as the entire course of the war. The Ground Troops would rely on strikes of strategic nuclear weapons and with the help of operational-tactical missiles would defeat the enemy's remaining forces (Kulikov 1976: 153, 160–61).

Despite the revolutionary changes in Soviet military doctrine and the ensuing revisions in the academy's curriculum (as well as the seeming irrelevance of the experience of past wars in these new conditions), the study of military history and the experience of the Great Patriotic War remained at the core of the academy's teaching program. Military historians on the faculty of the academy and in its research department focused their attention on the contribution of key operations of the Great Patriotic War to the development of the Soviet military art (Kulikov 1976: 162). In 1962—the period generally perceived as the height of the "revolution in military affairs"—the academic council of the academy decided to triple the amount of time allotted by the schedule to the teaching of the history of military art (from 58 hours to 190 hours) (Kulikov 1976: 166).

The evolution of Soviet military doctrine continued in the mid- and late 1960s and resulted in substantial changes in the views on the nature of a future war, which now allocated a much greater role to conventional weapons. Improvements in the capabilities of the Strategic Rocket Forces were paralleled by similar developments in conventional forces (Kulikov 1976: 179–80). The work of the academy followed this trend closely. The agenda was dominated by the issues of the conduct of nuclear and conventional operations and the problems of escalation (Kulikov 1976: 207).

The change in doctrine in the second half of the 1960s and renewed attention to conventional warfare apparently resulted in greater interest in military history and demand for military historians. In 1973, after a twenty-year interval, the history section was reestablished at the academy and the department of history of wars and military art was expanded. The new section was intended to train military historians for teaching and research posts at military academies and staff and Ministry of Defense assignments.[8]

The academy's research agenda in the second half of the 1960s and early 1970s reflected continuing interest in military history, especially the experience of the Great Patriotic War. For example, a study commissioned by the chief of the General Staff focused on the issue of the beginning period of war as it occurred in the past and in particular during World War II (Kulikov 1976: 209).

The academy also hosted a number of military-scientific conferences. In 1972 one such conference was held to commemorate the thirtieth anniversary of the Moscow battle and to discuss its significance for the development of Soviet military science. In his address to the conference head of the academy Army General Shavrov emphasized the continuing importance of the experience of the Great Patriotic War and the need to integrate its study with the teaching process: "History is a firm foundation for the development of military science and art. . . . [T]he study of the Great Patriotic War and the practical application of its experience is one of the most important tasks of Soviet military science" (Kulikov 1976: 210).

No subsequent changes in the academy's structure have taken place since the reestablishment of the military-historical section in

1973. Teaching and research have continued in step with the development of Soviet military doctrine, which was the principal factor that determined the course of the academy's work, and the growing importance of conventional warfare in the doctrine had affected the academy's agenda as well. The experience of the Great Patriotic War and subsequent local wars has continued to serve as the basis for new developments and improvements in contemporary military art. Its study has remained one of the key elements of the academy's teaching process (Kozlov 1987: 165–66).

One important detail that has not been mentioned so far in this survey of the postwar evolution of the General Staff Academy is that many members of its teaching and research staff have been trained and received advanced degrees in military history. In addition, they belonged to the generation that had seen combat duty during the war. It was the single most important event that shaped their professional outlook. A strong contingent of military historians has existed at the academy throughout its postwar development, and their expertise has not been limited to issues of military history alone (Kozlov 1987: 116; Kulikov 1976: 189). Thus, the heavy emphasis the academy places on military history, in particular that of the Great Patriotic War, has been supplemented and magnified by a teaching and research staff that has an inherent propensity to regard the study of the Great Patriotic War as central to the shaping of the military mind and the development of skills necessary for military professionals.

Conclusion

The two editions that cover the history of the General Staff Academy, as well as other sources cited in this chapter, provide convincing evidence in support of the present interpretation of the three functions of military history in the Soviet Union and its influence on Soviet military thinking. The description of the teaching process at the General Staff Academy and its research agenda, as well as their postwar evolution, has confirmed the argument concerning two functions of military history—the objective historical and the scientific-pedagogical—advanced earlier in this chapter. The strong presence of military history among the principal subjects at the academy, which prepares officers for positions in the senior echelons in the Soviet armed forces, in itself provides a good illustration of the objective historical and the scientific-pedagogical functions. The study of military history that focuses on the experience of the Great Patriotic War has been a key aspect of the training process at the academy from the immediate postwar years through the revolution in military affairs and to the present. Even when the experience of the Great Patriotic War and its lessons seemed of little or no relevance in the prevailing doctrinal context, they continued to occupy an important place in the academy's curriculum. The single most important reason for the emphasis given to the war experience was that the previous war was the only precedent the Soviet army could turn to in search of answers to questions posed by the advent of nuclear weapons and their impact on the conduct of a future war.

Naturally, evidence in support of the argument concerning the third function of military history—a discreet medium for surrogate discussions of current issues—could not be found in the two editions of the history of the General Staff Academy. A comparison of the 1976 and the 1987 editions and the discrepancies between them, however, suggests that military history serves as a medium for internal discussions within the Soviet military establishment.

Subtle and often rather obvious alterations of historical records reflect changes in doctrinal thinking. The 1976 edition of the book contained a rather long and thorough narrative of the teaching and research work carried out at the academy in the second half of the 1950s and 1960s when Soviet military doctrine was going through the stage known as the "revolution in military affairs" (Kulikov 1976: 141–68). The account reflected unequivocally the interest in nuclear weapons and the dominant role they played during that period, as well as their impact on Soviet military doctrine and thinking about the nature of a future war. In particular, the authors of the 1976 edition focused on Marshal Sokolovskii's 1959 lecture given before the academy's staff and students. As was mentioned earlier, the lecture has been cited as the turning point in the work of the academy—which subsequently devoted more time to the problems of nuclear war fighting (Kulikov 1976: 152–54).

By contrast, the 1987 edition of *Akademiya general'nogo shtaba* almost ignored this major event in the history of the academy. Sokolovskii's lecture was cited only briefly. The 1976 edition contained an extensive account of strategic and operational ideas involving massive use of nuclear weapons, which underlay the academy's teaching and research agenda during the revolution in military affairs. The 1987 edition described that period only in general terms and avoided specific mention of the content of the academy's curriculum.[9] The change reflects a clear and unequivocal desire to de-emphasize the nuclear stage in the evolution of Soviet military doctrine and the work of the General Staff Academy because it was inconsistent with contemporary Soviet military doctrine, which has long since moved toward a more conventional posture.[10]

Military history and in particular the history of the Great Patriotic War is likely to continue to serve its threefold function in the Soviet Union for the foreseeable future. The recent article by A. Kokoshin and V. Larionov discussed in the beginning of this chapter is just one example of the use of the history of the Great Patriotic War in the debate about doctrine and strategy that is currently underway in the Soviet Union.

A two-front war in Europe and the Far East will remain the top contingency facing the Soviet armed forces despite the changes in East-West relations, the signing of the INF Treaty, and the prospect of potentially more fruitful negotiations in the area of conventional arms control. The relevance of military history and World War II experience is not likely to diminish in the eyes of the Soviet defense establishment. On the contrary, perceptions of the increasing military uselessness of nuclear weapons will guarantee that Soviet defense planners will be even more preoccupied with conventional rather than nuclear operations than they have been in the last fifteen to twenty years. These developments will further enhance the practical value of and attention to the experience of the Great Patriotic War.

Even if in an era of greater openness internal discussions are brought out more into the public arena and military history loses its role as a medium for internal debates, its overall importance is not likely to diminish. Military history has become an integral part of an important and ongoing debate.

Notes

This chapter is based on a larger study sponsored by the Office of Net Assessment, U.S. Department of Defense, conducted at the Soviet Security Studies Working

Group at the Center for International Studies, MIT. The views expressed in this chapter are those of the author.

1   These suggestions did not go unnoticed. Articles that have appeared in *Voenno-istoricheskii zhurnal'* (*Military-historical journal*)—the leading periodical devoted to problems of military history in the USSR—since the publication of material criticizing military historians have addressed many of these subjects (Kotenev 1987: 59–64; Zavgorodniy 1987: 68–72; Khor'kov 1987: 15–24; Danilov 1987: 25–30; Ivashov 1987: 38–45; Babich 1987: 62–67).

2   The meeting was attended by such prominent members of the Soviet military and political establishment as Colonel General D. Volkogonov, deputy chief of the Main Political Administration; Colonel General M. Gareyev, deputy chief of the General Staff; Lieutenant General Ye. Kuznetsov, chief of the Military Science Administration of the General Staff; D. Kuznetsov, chief of the history sector in the Central Committee Science Department. The list of speakers included such distinguished names as Lieutenant General and Doctor of Military Science M. Kir'yan; Colonel A. Khor'kov, recently appointed to the post of the editor-in-chief of *Voenno-istoricheskii zhurnal'* (*Krasnaya zvezda* [*Red star*] 1987: 3; Krikunov and Pestov 1987: 12–16).

3   These functions are connected to and to some extent derived from each other. Therefore the division may appear somewhat artificial.

4   The novelty of this event was not only in the reinterpretation of the battle itself. The rewriting of history is not a new phenomenon in the Soviet Union. The sensation was caused by the fact that the article constituted the first foray in recent Soviet history by a civilian analyst into matters of military art—an area that until then had remained an exclusive province of military professionals.

    The most peculiar aspect of this incident was Kokoshin and Larionov's choice of a military historical discussion as the setting for a challenge to Soviet strategic thinking. The fact that Kokoshin and Larionov's attack on the professional military establishment, published in a civilian journal, was launched in the form of revision of lessons of a key World War II battle is highly telling of the degree to which military history has permeated Soviet military thinking and defined the terms for Soviet military strategic discourse.

5   As is shown elsewhere in this volume, the continuity of Soviet armed forces' strategic mission in the Eurasian continent and the experience of World War II have been key factors in Soviet postwar military development.

6   *Voenny entsiklopedicheskii slovar'* 1986: 135–36.

7   An incident described by General P. Grigorenko in his memoirs offers a good illustration of the impact of history on the thinking of a well-educated Soviet career military officer.

    Upon his arrival to the Far East in 1939 at the time of the Soviet-Japanese conflict Grigorenko—a recent graduate of the General Staff Academy—was assigned to the staff of Marshall G. Zhukov. Having acquainted himself with the operational situation, Grigorenko realized that the troops under Zhukov's command were waging a campaign that was nearly identical to the disastrous experience of the Russian army led by General Kuropatkin during the course of the Russo-Japanese War of 1904–5.

At this point I recalled the Russo-Japanese War experience of commander Kuropatkin. . . . Every experienced officer was familiar with Kuropatkin's tactic. It had been so caustically ridiculed in the literature of military history that it was hard to imagine anyone would ever repeat it. But Zhukov, who had never studied in the academy and who evidently had never studied the lessons of the Russo-Japanese War, was following Kuropatkin's methods exactly. (Grigorenko 1982: 106–7)

8   Kulikov 1976: 190, 202. Its predecessor—the military-historical faculty—was disbanded in 1953.

9   Kozlov 1987: 119–20. The apparent discomfort of the authors of the 1987 edition of the book with early Soviet views on nuclear weapons and the desire to dismiss them as immature can be seen in the following passage:

The seminars were used to raise the most complex issues which required creative discussion and for which definitive solutions had to be worked out.

The [academy's] instructors themselves learned a lot at these seminars since in fact they were in the same conditions as the students. Neither the instructors nor the students had the necessary knowledge about the new weapons and methods of their use. (Kozlov 1987: 120)

10   An interesting disavowal of early Soviet thinking about nuclear weapons can be found in Marshal N. Ogarkov's 1985 booklet *Istoriya uchit bditel'nosti* (*History teaches vigilance*):

The development of new weapons and military equipment leads to qualitative changes in the methods of warfare. But this does not happen immediately when the weapons are developed, but only when they are used in quantities [sufficient to produce] a [qualitative change]. . . .

In the 50's and 60's when there were few nuclear weapons they were considered as a means of enhancing sharply the firepower of troops. All kinds of attempts were made to adapt [nuclear weapons] to the then-existing forms of warfare and first and foremost for accomplishing strategic missions. Subsequently in the 70's and 80's rapid qualitative changes in nuclear weapons of varying yields and the development of various long-range and highly accurate means of delivery and its widespread deployment . . . resulted in a radical revision of earlier views on the role of these weapons. (Ogarkov 1985: 50–51)

3

Soviet Staff Structure and Planning in World War II

Condoleezza Rice

The ability of the Soviet command to reverse their catastrophic failures at the beginning of World War II stands as one of the most remarkable turnarounds in modern military history. A number of explanations can be given for the eleventh hour reversal. One could point, for example, to the errors of the German command, the revision of Soviet strategy and tactics to take better account of the potential for defensive operations, or the improvements in Soviet equipment and weaponry.

The Soviets also managed to create rather quickly organizations of strategic leadership (*strategicheskoe rukovodst'vo*), like the GKO (State Defense Committee) and STAVKA (Supreme High Command of the Armed Forces), which ultimately led to successful mobilization and direction of resources. But there were also important improvements at the level of troop control (*upravleniye voiskam*); in the organization of the General Staff itself and in its relationship to subordinate staffs at the operational level. Co-ordination with service staffs improved as well, strengthening combined arms operations.

The Soviets themselves have tended to concentrate on telling the stories of success at higher levels of leadership. But there have been a few recent works and articles that give an increasingly clear picture of the relationship at lower levels. This chapter explores some of the changes that were made in the organization of the work of the General Staff organization and in its relationship to service staffs and to field staffs at subordinate levels.

As with everything else about the Soviet war effort, staff work in the period from June 1941 until the successful defense of Moscow was marked by chaos and confusion. The Soviets were simply trying to survive, and organizational arrangements were created and abandoned with great rapidity. The staffs, more often than not, employed ad hoc means to overcome deficiencies in communication and planning.

But with the successful defense of Moscow and the accumulating wartime experience work became more routinized as a functioning staff system evolved. This is not to say that it always operated smoothly, but by the time of the Battle of Stalingrad, the staff system was operating well enough to support the more demanding tasks of offensive operations.

The Internal Organization of the General Staff

One of the most difficult problems for a military staff is to make a smooth transition from its peacetime to its wartime role. The greatest challenge, of course, is in the period of crisis, when the staff must provide the political leadership with intelligence estimates of enemy strength and preparation and assessments of the likely direction and timing of attack. Given the initial German successes and the well-chronicled failure of the Soviet leadership to prepare adequately for the attack, some blame must be cast upon the General Staff.[1]

Obviously, there were mitigating circumstances. The role of Josef Stalin in refusing to accept the inevitability of the German attack ranks as one of the most egregious failures to read strategic warning in modern history. Moreover, the Great Purges are certainly to blame for the cowardly and disorganized fashion in which the General Staff occasionally performed. Nevertheless, even with these caveats, more recent Soviet historiography suggests that the General Staff was also mistaken in its expectations about the character of the initial period of the war.

In the spring of 1941 the General Staff drafted a plan of defense that employed only skeletal forces at the frontier (Shtemenko 1981:

26). The staff assumed that the German offensive would be preceded by operations of a limited character, allowing the bulk of Soviet forces time to take up their defensive positions. Thus the main forces of the Soviet Union were to be deployed as much as 100 kilometers from the frontier. B. M. Shtemenko, a member of the General Staff at the time, has attempted to justify this plan, suggesting that "echeloning" of forces in depth is a concept well proven in military history. He also states that the General Staff correctly identified the most dangerous enemy and the overall character of the war.

But on the key elements of the timing of the attack and its intensity, the General Staff was clearly wrong. Students of the "initial period of the war" have blamed the errors on assumptions derived from World War I: the General Staff assumed that there would be a period of mobilization of enemy forces. They believed that at most, an unmobilized Germany could mount only initial operations, giving Soviet forces time to redeploy. There was no recognition that the Phony War had placed Germany on war footing and that the Wehrmacht was thus ready to proceed from a standing start (Ivanov 1971). In short, Stalin was not the only one to underestimate the importance of surprise; and the combined impact of his underestimate and of an existing General Staff plan that underestimated surprise undoubtedly contributed to Stalin's refusal to believe the irrefutable evidence of German preparations that he was soon to receive.

Even this miscalculation does not account for the refusal to read the signs of warning. It is, of course, questionable whether Stalin would have believed any evidence of the inevitability of the German attack. Most Soviet and Western historiography suggests that he would not have. But whatever the answer to that question, the General Staff did not help the situation. Poorly organized internally to exploit reconnaissance and intelligence, General Staff reports on German preparations were tentative at best. Golikov, perhaps for his own protection, tended to give raw intelligence reports and there was little effort to collate the findings into anything approximating analysis. Moreover, Golikov was given to separating intelligence into "reliable" and "doubtful." By many accounts, the separation was based mainly on Golikov's attempt to tell Stalin what he wanted to hear.[2] Warnings from commanders in the field were given as seriatim, which undoubtedly blunted their impact. In short, if a coherent picture of an imminent attack was forming it was certainly not due to the efforts of the GRU (or Main Directorate for Intelligence). Any preparations that were taken by commanders in the field, and there were some, were taken largely in spite of, not at the behest of, the General Staff.

Once the war began, the problem of reconnaissance and intelligence reporting worsened for a while until organizational means were developed. In some cases the major struggle was to get any information from the field. In others there were conflicting assessments.

Front commanders were to report at least twice a day both the combat situation and any information on the disposition of German forces. While obviously these reports would be most useful for the General Staff, they were difficult to obtain in the early days of the war because of the instability of communications.[3] The rampant confusion at the outset of the war led to numerous conditions in which the General Staff issued orders to armies that had long since been overrun.

A second source of information were reports about the situation from Party organizations, both civilian and military. According to B. M. Shtemenko, a former chief of the general staff, the reports from these sources were often found to be exaggerated in one direction or another (Shtemenko 1981). Exaggerated reports about the strength of resistance on the first day of the invasion from the Party organizations on the Western front probably delayed the decision to order retreat in some cases. On the other hand, the military council of the southwestern military district correctly reported the deteriorating conditions for forces in Kiev and requested permission to retreat. Stalin refused, however, relying instead on exaggerated reports of staunch resistance from other unnamed Party sources. Clearly, conflicting reports from the field were a major problem in devising operational strategy in Moscow.

Eventually, with communications still unstable, the General Staff had to find the means for securing reliable information as well as the means for verifying implementation of orders. For the first task the staff organized its own reconnaissance missions to key sectors, sometimes making several reconnaissance flight or ground patrols per week. These were not without cost, however. So many officers were out on reconnaissance that the other functions, such as military planning and intelligence assessment, suffered. While the officers "roved about in SB and PO-2 aircraft," they might have been gathering important information but there were too few officers back at headquarters planning operations (Shtemenko 1981: 47). These reconnaissance flights were quite dangerous. A number of staff officers were shot down and killed or captured. Or, conversely, sometimes officers who were sent out on patrol arrived at front or army headquarters only to be pressed into service by the commander, also short of staff officers.

Obviously, something had to be done to routinize reconnaissance and intelligence. First, the operations department developed better ties with the intelligence directorate for effective exchange of information. Daily intelligence briefings for the chief of operations and his deputies were instituted. Second, coordination of both intelligence and reporting concerning the combat situation and the disposition of Soviet troops was organized by geographic branches in August 1941. This structure was soon found wanting, however, and the branches were abandoned in favor of officers assigned to monitor specific fronts. Eventually, teams of General Staff officers with specific responsibilities (transport, intelligence, readiness of reserves, and so on) were developed for each front (Shtemenko 1981: 247).

Assessment of battle conditions as well as verification of order implementation were made easier by the creation of a group of liaison officers from the General Staff to the front and army levels, called the Officer Corps of the General Staff. Initially, these officers worked for the operations department and returned frequently to Moscow to resume duties on the General Staff (Saltyikov 1971: 54). Eventually, they were made independent of the operations department and reported directly to the chief of the General Staff, and remained with the front and army command. In some geographic sectors these officers were deployed down to the corps and division level.

These liaison officers were subordinate only to the General Staff officer at the next level. For instance, an officer at the army level was subordinate to the General Staff corps officer at the front, and so on. In the early days of the war the officer, like the commander, made daily reports to the chief of the General Staff on the basis "only of what he had seen with his own eyes; he was not allowed to quote other people or headquarters documents." The function of the officer corps was soon downgraded, however. The sheer volume of reports to Moscow and the ire of commanders who felt that the alternative chain was inappropriate forced a change. Within a few months, the liaison officers no longer reported on the current situation but were to give the General Staff views of longer term trends. As communications stabilized and the course of the war turned toward the Soviets, the officer corps became less and less important. Eventually, in 1943 they were transferred back to the operations department and were relegated to less central tasks. They participated heavily, for instance, in the work associated with the formation of the Czech and Polish corps after 1943.

Nonetheless, the officer corps did serve as a source of battle experience for many officers who returned to the General Staff proper. It was also an important temporary measure during the days when assessing the situation at the front was a source of considerable concern.

Though Stalin apparently preferred firsthand verification of the situation at the front, the stabilization of the communications situation allowed the General Staff to rely increasingly on technical means to stay abreast of conditions.

At the outset of the war the General Staff suffered from the lack of a complete network of communications and from the instability of those that were in operation. The General Staff was heavily dependent on a single communications network center through which all radio, telephone and telegraphic communication was transmitted (Perespyipkin 1971: 19). In the early days of the war transmission was not only unreliable due to disruption but also jammed with attempts to get through from multiple fronts. A special communications line "BODO" connected the leadership and STAVKA, located in the Kremlin, and the General Staff headquarters. On June 24, 1941 hurriedly developed networks were established between the General Staff and the major fronts (northern, northwestern, and so on) as well. But in all cases, these were primarily telegraph and in some cases telephone lines, both of which were still subject to disruption and were often overloaded.

Slowly, as the military situation allowed, land lines were added to the communications network. The first functioning ones linked the STAVKA reserves with the General Staff. Others soon followed and eventually the network was complete enough to allow the General Staff skip echelon communications to the army level, or in some cases, to the corps level. Additionally, service headquarters and reserve networks were developed linking alternative as well as primary command posts.

An interesting question is why the General Staff's communications network was so rudimentary at the beginning of the war. A communications directorate was created for the General Staff in the reorganization of 1935, but the staff was extremely dependent on the People's Commissariat for Communication. It is possible that the Soviets had simply devoted too little money to building the communications network. There is, however, at least one suggestion that there may have also been concerns about political control. The concerns were particularly strong concerning skip echelon communications that would allow the General Staff to pass orders to the army or, in some cases, corps levels.

The problem of linking the General Staff to the field was not a new one.[4] At the time of the Civil War one of the biggest problems had been communication with the front and the rudimentary system of communications that existed at the time. In 1918 this could certainly be blamed on the underdeveloped state of Russia. But in examining the problem of military leadership and the functions of a military staff in the period from 1918 to 1924, concerns surfaced about allowing a separate set of communications networks for the military. As early as 1918 a number of articles focused on the pernicious effect that the notorious German General Staff communications channel had on civilian control at the outset of World War I.[5] The German General Staff had employed direct communications to field commanders (circumventing even field staffs), apparently as a means of issuing orders without political authority.

We do not know what means of political control accompanied the eventual solution of the communications problem in the direction of military centralization. The General Staff finally acquired its skip echelon communications and means of direct communication with the field by alternative means. It should be noted, though, that STAVKA and with it, Stalin, was also outfitted with direct means of communication to the field.[6] These links were apparently used often as the generalissimo was known to occasionally and apparently randomly call field commanders for personal reports on the situation.

Improved communication made the job of the General Staff much easier in matters of planning because it could now be reasonably certain that it was planning on the basis of reliable information. Concurrently, methods of planning and coordination were improving as well.

First, the staff organization was standardized within the directorates of the General Staff, the service staffs, and at every level throughout the armed forces. In retrospect, it is surprising that there was so much variation throughout the system prior to World War II. It is important to remember, though, that staff structure had been in flux from the time of the revolution. Indecision, primarily political, concerning whether the Soviet Union should have a General Staff meant that from 1918 to 1935 there were constant reforms and counterreforms. The Soviets could not decide how centralized military planning should be.

While issues of military science (debate about the character of future war) were considered the legitimate domain of the military staff almost from inception, other issues like the role of the staff in mobilization and training, reconnaissance and intelligence, communications and, finally, the character of its wartime role, were constantly changing (Rice 1987).

The initial Red Army Staff organization closely resembled that of the Russian Imperial Staff or the German General Staff. But after the Civil War the debate entitled "Shall We Have A General Staff?" intensified. Clearly, the concern was political. The Soviets were haunted by the image of the political role of the German General Staff. The Frunze reforms of 1924–25 strengthened the staff's role in the development of military thought but distributed other functions, including a role in "economic issues," to civilian bodies. The staff was given an operations directorate to oversee battlefield developments but without communications, intelligence, and responsibility for mobilization and training of reserves, it would have been difficult for the staff to have carried out these functions. The solution seems to have been something of a compromise because there were those who actually wanted a civilian body to parallel the function of the General Staff. Since it was thought, however, that this might cause disruptions in strategic planning, the suggestion was dropped. Nonetheless, the General Staff's role fell far short of the rather comprehensive view that was held by some who had hoped that it might be accorded a role in drafting economic plans. The possibility of the General Staff as a command staff (as had been the German model) with the right to issue orders in its name was never at issue. The Soviet General Staff was then and is now only able to pass orders signed by the commander in chief of STAVKA.

The reforms of 1935 rounded out the functions of the General Staff, giving it some of the functions for training, mobilization, and intelligence that it had lost in the Frunze reforms. But the Great Purges retarded the development of the organizational structure of the General Staff. What is quite clear about the Finnish campaign is that the General Staff was completely unable to function in support of commanders in the field. It appears to have been, in some cases, almost superfluous.

At the outset of the war there were numerous organizations that shared responsibility with the General Staff for key functions. A problem existed between the General Staff and an organization that was given responsibility for mobilizing and training forces (GLAVUPRAFORM). Eventually, the situation between the two organizations became so bad that Stalin personally delineated their functions. But the problem could not be solved in that way and GLAVUPRAFORM was ultimately disbanded and its functions were given back to the General Staff. The General Staff now had primary responsibility for mobilization and allocation of reserves, always, of course, under the watchful eye of STAVKA and Stalin, in whose name those orders were given.

In short, the lack of standarized organization throughout the system at the beginning of the war was probably a result of ambivalence about the organization of the General Staff itself. Slowly, a standard organization did evolve. By 1942 staffs throughout the system were similarly organized with the operations directorate at the core.[7]

The operations directorate, the nerve center of any military staff, was responsible for daily reports to the command. STAVKA was the highest level to which reports were made, and at subordinate levels the reports were made to the commander. At each level the chief operations officer was deputy chief of staff and was the only officer with direct access to the chief of staff. Operations officers collected and processed intelligence information about the enemy, assessed the strength of the fronts and the conditions of reserves.

At the General Staff there were for each region sector chiefs who oversaw teams of officers who held the responsibility for fronts. There were also functionally responsible deputy chiefs. For example, one deputy chief had direct responsibility for the organizational structure of the arms of the services. He also planned the buildup of fronts, handled the distribution of troops in the military districts, and dealt with military training establishments to assure a steady supply of officers. Eventually this deputy chief was also placed in charge of military transport, which at other times during the war was under the General Staff or the chief of logistics, who was simultaneously People's Commissar for Railways. The decision to unify under one authority all matters of troop distribution, training, and movement is judged by at least one author to have been very successful.

The operations department of the General Staff not only staffed the chief of the General Staff but apparently kept direct contact with the operations department of the front, and in some cases, the army level. On each staff at subordinate levels the minimum number of operations officers was two (this number was of course much larger in higher level staffs), one dealt with information and one directed operations. The breakdown of staff structure at the corps level, for example, was as follows:

Staff of Corps in 1941

Operations	10
Intelligence	4
Communications	5
Rear Services	3

Staff functions were further delineated and by the end of the war rear services had been removed and replaced by a second communications section, which also handled transportation of forces.

Staff of Corps in 1945

Operations	6
Intelligence	5
Communications	3
Communications and Transportation	4
Personnel	4
Special	4

This more standardized and smoothly coordinated staff structure facilitated both information flow and operational planning (Pope 1974: 28). Clearly, the operations departments of subordinate staffs were busy drafting suggestions from their commanders to the General Staff for operational concepts. The General Staff solicited, and sometimes received unsolicited, commanders' ideas in planning operations.

Final authority rested with STAVKA, but in its role of drafting options, especially at the conceptual stage, the General Staff counted heavily on the front commander's intimate knowledge of his troops and the situation on the ground. This is not to say that the General Staff was overly dependent on commanders for the concept. The multiplicity of channels from which suggestions were received, military councils, party workers, service staffs, is evident throughout the literature. But special authority was accorded the commander's suggestions.

According to Soviet sources, an operational plan begins with a concept that is developed to determine the main goal. The strength of one's own and one's enemy's forces is assessed to determine a weak point at which the enemy can be defeated. If experience from other campaigns is relevant, it is factored in. The General Staff and all subordinate staffs maintained departments for the "usage of the experience of the war" whose purpose was to give substance to prior experience. The academies also conducted ongoing games and research on improving the outcomes of past battles (see also Kulikov 1974: 74–78).

The next step was to determine the timing of the attack. How important was speed, surprise? This in part led to a solution of the next issue, that of means. For example, how important was mobility? Finally, support and logistics for the plan needed to be examined. At that point an operational plan was ready for discussion and/or approval by STAVKA so that an implementing order could be approved.

But clearly the process was quite interactive, involving the operations departments of the subordinate units. For purposes of illustration, let us digress and examine how the plan for the defeat of occupying forces in Belorussia was developed. It shows that while STAVKA was certainly the final locus of considerable discussion and of the resulting decision, the relationship between the operations department of the General Staff and of Rokossovsky's front command and staff was also key.

At the beginning of 1944 the General Staff assessed the overall situation and decided that the main thrust of the summer campaign should be toward Nazi forces in and around Belorussia (see Shtemenko 1981:319). "A major victory would bring Soviet troops to the vital frontiers of the Third Reich by the shortest possible route." Several concepts were received from the front, but Rokossovsky's plan for a two-stage operation using concentration of force at one point on the front caught the eye of the General Staff. Having weakened the German forces at "their heart and brain," all forces of the front would rout flank concentrations. The plan, although thought to be brilliant, was also risky. It was also decided that not enough force could be concentrated in the first stage of the assault. Rokossovsky's proposed concentrated offensive through Kovel was rejected but a curtailed version of the operation was adopted.

The key to the operation was believed to be speed and extreme secrecy. Deceptive measures were taken to convince the German command that the thrust was coming in the Baltic area. Detailed instructions were sent to the Baltic region to prepare offensive operations under operational camouflage. The forces at the Baltic fronts, not knowing themselves that these were measures to deceive the Germans, carried out preparations. This carefully prepared deception was successful in diverting German attention.

Meanwhile, Rokossovsky was consulted again about an operational plan based on the revised concept. He made known that he attached particular importance to the continuity of the offensive. Speed was very important and there should be no delay in the arrival of the tank corps supporting army operations. Rokossovsky's concept of splitting the enemy into two parts was accepted. The General Staff solved the problem of momentum by deciding to commit a tank army to improve the mobility of the forces in the operation.

This plan was then taken to STAVKA, where it was discussed for two days. STAVKA adjusted the plan, making, for instance, a decision that the breakthrough would be exploited by encircling the German forces. An operational order was prepared. When the directive concerning the offensive had been sent, the STAVKA representatives set out for the fronts. They went to the fronts to make sure that the front commanders understood the orders and to provide coordination among the fronts. They were also to assure logistical support.

While not all commanders' concepts were suggested, it is clear the operational planning process was quite interactive. According to most accounts, this interactive quality of planning improved as the war wore on. But interestingly, there are also veiled references that, as victory neared, front commanders became increasingly concerned with the importance of the missions to which they were attached. So, for instance, when the planning for the capture of Berlin began, every commander wanted to share in that symbolic as well as important military victory. Here the General Staff was aided by Stalin's solutions. "Let the first to break through take Berlin." And, "Just be sure that if the Western allies show any progress toward Berlin that you move for it" (Shtemenko 1981). From that point on it appears that commanders were in competition with each other to deliver the final blow and to seal the victory of the Soviet Union in World War II.

Combined Arms Cooperation

The other major concern for the General Staff was coordination with service staffs. Though the Soviets tout the success of their combined arms operations, constant admonition to solve the problem of combining all arms of the services, suggests that a solution to the problem has always been elusive.

Such was the case in World War II. The problems in combining air and ground forces became especially acute after the Soviets went over to the general offensive in 1943. In general, it was the responsibility of the air staff to assess the effectiveness of aviation at the front. At the beginning of the war the air staff, like everything else in the Soviet army, was not particularly well organized. Due to severe understaffing, officers were required to do several jobs simultaneously. Eventually, a number of air officers were brought back from the field and two officers each were allocated at the central and front levels for (1) assessing the composition of air forces, (2) preparing operational orders that were delivered to the General Staff's operational department three times a day, and (3) examining maps and assessing the situation in the air. Additionally, an information control officer was designated so that the chief of staff would not be overwhelmed and a chief of the rear for VVS (Army Air Forces) was appointed and given a small staff

war or whether the foregoing can be relegated to the category of interesting but now irrelevant history. Within a few years of the end of the war the demands of postwar planning and command were complicated and, in some cases, radically altered by the full-scale incorporation of nuclear weapons.

Indeed the Soviets speak of the revolution in military affairs brought about by nuclear weapons as having a third stage: coping with the problems of command and control. Given the rapidity with which battlefield conditions would change, the speed of modern weaponry also probably makes obsolete the World War II pace of staff work.

Nonetheless, several key tenets have survived from the experience of World War II. First, the General Staff's structure and its relationship to field staffs, which creates a seamless web of communications networks and planning structures from the central level down to at least the division level, has not changed.

The Soviets also understand that problems can result from this centralization if commanders and their staffs lack initiative. Thus, the concept from World War II and from the German staff culture of the staff officer as the alter ego of the commander is emphasized in staff training. The commander and his chief of staff are expected to be so in tune with the concept of operation that the decisions taken, even without the intervention of the General Staff, will be supportive of the overall strategic plan.

In modern Soviet thinking great emphasis is also devoted to the development of combined arms staffs that truly understand how to obtain synergistic results between naval, air, and ground forces. As in World War II, the staffs seem to be better at ground-air coordination, but heavier reliance on well-staffed and well-commanded theaters of military operations has encouraged that trend.

In the final analysis, though, the centrality of troop control in Soviet military thought suggests that the Soviets understand better than any that it is at this level—between the center, the front, and subordinate units—that wars are won and lost. Much has been made of the failures of strategic leadership in the first days of the war and the successful reversal of those initial mistakes. But the improvements in troop control and coordination with the field were perhaps more a product of reorganizing relations from the General Staff level downward than the reverse. The Soviets believe that strategic planning assures tactical success. Communication and coordination with those in the field should have been at the core of Soviet prewar planning but they were not. Methods had to be invented in the course of war.

The great Soviet military thinker Mikhail Tukhachevskii once warned "It is better to predict than to learn from history." The failure to predict organizational forms and to carry through with their implementation almost resulted in the destruction of the Soviet Union. Fortunately from the Soviet point of view they reorganized and recovered in time to give themselves another chance.

Notes

1 Shtemenko 1981 is both the most authoritative and most apologetic source on the role of the General Staff in that period.
2 Golikov's role has become difficult to untangle from the trends in Soviet historiography that either vilify or glorify Stalin. Uncharitable accounts include Ivanov 1966. The most favorable account is an anonymous piece, Marshal 1980: 87, which gives Golikov credit for preparing the armed forces.
3 Erickson 1962 provides the most colorful and interesting account of this period.
4 A series of articles appeared in the first military daily *Armiya i flot rabochei i krestyanskoi Rossii*. See Goshcitskiyi 1917.
5 See for example *Voennoe delo*, 1 March 1920.
6 B. M. Shtemenko talks dispassionately about the active interventions of Stalin throughout his 1981 volume.
7 Three sources concerning the reorganization of the staffs and the key role played by operational departments are particularly helpful. See Shtemenko 1981, Kozhevnikov 1985, and Popel 1974.
8 Coordination with the navy is treated in Popel 1984.

Part II

World War II and the Present

4

Soviet Risk Taking in Major Crises in the Postwar Era

Jonathan R. Adelman

Soviet risk taking in the major crises of the postwar era is an important topic in international politics. In the first half of the twentieth century a strong propensity for risk taking by imperial Germany had helped bring on World War I and a powerful and even reckless desire for war by Nazi Germany and imperial Japan had led to World War II. Their zeal for war helped bring both states important early victories in both enormous conflagrations but in the long run they suffered final defeat at the hands of a broad and diverse alliance cemented by a desire to halt the aggressors. This reflected in large part the powerful disparity between the ultimate means available to the aggressors and the capacities of their enemies in the two wars (Voznesenskii 1948: 10; Vorontsov 1976: 110; and Aldcroft 1978: 110).

With the development of the cold war in the late 1940s, the issue of Soviet military power and risk taking became of central importance to Western policymakers. As I argue in a recent book, World War II had demonstrated the powerful role played by the Red Army in the defeat of Nazi Germany, hitherto the world's foremost military machine (Adelman 1988). The weaknesses of the Red Army were manifold and manifest—no strategic bomber force, a weak navy, merely adequate tactical air power, poorly educated manpower. Yet, for all these problems, it had borne the brunt of the war, suffering 7 million military fatalities and 5.5 million prisoners taken captive by the Germans, and had emerged victorious (Urlanis 1971: 209–10). At the end of the war the Red Army stood in Berlin, Prague, Vienna and Budapest, planning to divide Europe with the United States. Given the superiority and proximity of Soviet land power to Europe and Asia and the great difficulties the war had demonstrated in the projection of a more limited American land power on distant continents, the topic of Soviet risk taking became a central one.

The predominant view of the Soviet Union during the rise of the cold war explicitly equated the Soviet Union with Nazi Germany. The new "totalitarian" theorists, led by Zbigniew Brzezinski, Carl Friedrich and Hannah Arendt, saw the Soviet Union as the heir apparent to Nazi Germany and as even more dangerous than its predecessor, due to its broad ideological appeal. In their classic 1956 volume, *Totalitarian Dictatorship and Democracy*, Carl Friedrich and Zbigniew Brzezinski spoke of "the Soviet forward march" and saw the combination of communism and Russian imperialism as "providing the Russian imperial expansion with an ideological underpinning far more potent than the older Panslavist and Third Reich ideologies." Friedrich and Brzezinski made clear their view of Soviet risk taking when they declared:

> The struggle for world conquest . . . is the totalitarians' natural bent . . . extension of Soviet control over one bit of territory after another has been proceeding since 1945 with almost the annual regularity of the seasons. After the big grab of that first year netting Poland, Rumania, Hungary, and Jugoslavia, there have been the additions of Czechoslovakia, Eastern Germany, China, Korea, and now Indochina . . . it seems to be only a matter of time until the next victim is "bagged." . . . Any relaxation of the vigilance required to face such ideological imperialists as the totalitarians is likely to result in disasters such as the Second World War, or worse. (1961: 63, 65, 68)

In the early 1980s there was a resurgence in the popularity of the "totalitarian" theory, one coincident with the election of President Ronald Reagan in the United States.

This imagery and its popularity raises important questions for this chapter. First and foremost, what is the relationship between the World War II experience and Soviet behavior in major postwar crises? Secondly, what have been the general Soviet proclivities in such crises over time? In order to answer these questions we need to do several things. We need to define clearly the parameters of risk taking and the problems inherent in such analysis by Western scholars. We must review the extant literature on Soviet risk taking in major crises. Then we need to examine a series of Soviet decisions under such situations and the interaction of such crises and the World War II experience.

World War II promoted a strong Soviet reluctance to use force, given the high costs of war and its unpredictability. Only on its borders, whose importance had been shown so dramatically by the history of the war, was the Soviet Union willing to use force. The legacy of the past has led them to place great emphasis on preparation for war. The war experience only reinforced traditional views of the West as politically hostile and technologically highly capable. Overall, the war further reduced the Soviet interest in any foreign intervention in the postwar era.

Soviet Risk Taking

The decision on the use of major force in a crisis depends on both objective and subjective factors. Objectively, the Soviet Union, like any actor, needs to review the basic parameters of the situation, involving the military, economic, political and cultural factors that can be placed in any correlation-of-forces calculus. The regular bureaucratic problems of information processing, ideology, and structure exist throughout the process. There are also specific factors associated with crises that may induce distortions in the data available to the leaders. This points to the subjective factors that come into play especially when time becomes short, information limited, and relationships complex. Risk awareness may become as important as objective risks.

Hannes Adomeit (1982) has well identified the subjective factors in Soviet decision making. It then becomes precisely the "perceptions of the adversary's risk-taking propensities, his priorities and commitments and on mutual expectations and beliefs about probable responses and counteractions" that count heavily (1982: 3–11). In process analysis we look at the variety of options perceived to be available to the leaders, the relationship between verbal and actual behavior, the risk thresholds and degree of acceptance of rules of the game. In analyzing the factors of behavior we look at the role of ideology, security factors, the role of balance of interest versus balance of power, the correlation between aspects of military balance and the propensity of risk taking and the role of the dominant leader, the power struggle and the institutional conflict on behavior. The main factors of risk taking are usually seen by most analyses as ideology, security and state interests, military power and domestic influences on individual, group, and systemic levels.

Problems of Analysis

There are serious problems in conducting any analysis of Soviet risk taking. An analysis of risk taking in Western countries can draw on a plethora of information that is unavailable in the Soviet case. The lack of reliable information can be daunting. Scholars have no access to Politburo leaders and key officials, who cannot be interviewed, never publicly reveal their own positions or write candid memoirs. There are no presidential libraries or freedom of information acts to ultimately open all archival material to scholars. There is no access to Politburo minutes or records of debates at top levels. There is no free press to leak key material on the stance of various leaders and the nature and extent of their disagreements.

The views and motivations of individual leaders and the nature and extent of their alliances can only be guessed at in the West. While such information on Western leaders is public knowledge, Western scholars often argue over the actual stance and relationship of various Soviet leaders on key issues. Thus, for example, Robert Slusser and Hannes Adomeit are in basic dispute not simply about the interpretation but even about the facts of the 1961 Berlin crisis (Slusser 1973; Adomeit 1982). This also reflects not only a difficulty in agreeing on facts but also a divergence in value orientation and analytic tools used by Western scholars. In particular, there is a sharp difference between scholars committed to a bureaucratic politics approach (such as Valenta, Slusser and Rice) and those more oriented to a rational actor, unified approach (such as Adomeit and Dawisha).[1]

There is also a sharp disagreement among Western analysts about the proper model to use in evaluating and conceiving Soviet foreign policy decision making.[2]

Literature

Under these conditions it will be hardly surprising for the reader to learn of the general inadequacy of the extant literature on Soviet crisis decision making. In 1973 a study by Arnold Horelick, A. Ross Johnson, and John Steinbruner for the RAND Corporation found that unlike the literature of the American foreign policy field, the literature on Soviet foreign policy cases was "small, fragmented and generally underdeveloped" (1973: 41). More recently, Hannes Adomeit has complained of the "widely scattered" nature of the field and the "curious" lack of concern for cumulation in the field (1982:4). Although there has been some progress in the 1980s, these problems essentially remain. There has been no successful integration of the various case studies in the field. And there is a serious lack of comparability and cumulation among the scattered and dispersed case studies.

The one area of progress has been in the number of such studies. Nearly all of the major crises of the postwar era now have at least one, or occasionally, as in the case of Berlin 1961 and Czechoslovakia 1968, two studies of Soviet decision making devoted to them. Although there is no richness of available material, there is at least some base on which to erect a broader study of Soviet crisis decision making.[3] Furthermore, Stephen Kaplan's study of the Soviet armed forces as a political instrument does provide some quantitative basis for a broader study (1981). Indeed, in a forthcoming volume I will essay such an overview (1990).

Nevertheless, it is important to remember that the overall literature in the field remains quite weak. It is plagued also by sharp conflicts in values between various authors. Even the groundwork of any study, the systematic description of events, remains weak. For as Hannes Adomeit recently complained, "Surprisingly, systematic compilations and description of data are, to say the least, weak. This is indeed surprising given that the 'Why?' questions cannot be answered at all without defining what precisely it is that needs to be answered" (1986: 11). Given the great importance of Soviet intervention decisions in the postwar era, it is still a bit disconcerting to realize how weak the literature remains on this vital topic.

The extant literature basically stresses the very cautious and conservative nature of the Soviet use of force. Contrary to the images conjured up by "totalitarian" theorists, there has been no generally aggressive use of force or expansionism by the Soviet Union. The proper analogy to the Soviet use of force has been not that of Nazi Germany but that of any of the great traditional European powers before 1914.

The Impact of World War II on Soviet Risk Taking

Far from embodying the totalitarian images, the Soviet Union has generally acted in a very cautious and conservative manner in the postwar era. Except for the intervention in Afghanistan in 1979, the Soviet Union has eschewed the massive application of force in any region outside of the Warsaw Pact. Even there the large-scale use of force has been far from automatic. In Poland in 1956 and again in 1980 and 1981, the Soviet Union did not use its army to crush significant opposition. It tolerated the Yugoslav deviation after 1948 and the Rumanian deviation after the middle 1960s without resorting to force. Even when it did use force in Hungary in 1956 and Czechoslovakia in 1968 it did so only after considerable hesitation and a search for alternative means to resolve the crisis. In Poland from August 1980 until December 1981 it tolerated the heterodoxy of Solidarity and then through martial law it found an internal Polish remedy to resolve the crisis.

Outside the bloc Russia's only major use of force came in Afghanistan, which saw a Communist regime come to power in 1978, and where there was no likelihood of Western military intervention in a traditionally pro-Soviet neutral country on the Soviet border. There were numerous opportunities for the massive application of growing Soviet military power in the postwar era. The Soviet Union supported Cuban interventions in Africa in the 1970s, heavily armed its Middle Eastern supporters, and even flew combat missions and manned air defense systems in Egypt in the early 1970s. But the overall gap between the great and expanding conventional military power of the Soviet Union and its extreme reluctance to utilize that power outside the bloc (especially compared to the much more frequent use of American military power) was wide and growing in the postwar era. In this chapter I wish to speculate on possible causes for this behavior.

World War II, of course, remains only one possible explanation for Soviet behavior. After all, it can be argued that the Soviet Union, especially since the failed counteroffensive in Poland in 1920, has traditionally been a very cautious and conservative military power. This was already evident before 1945. In March 1918 Lenin paid a huge price in the onerous Treaty of Brest-Litovsk in order to remove the Soviet Union from a debilitating war. At the end of the civil war in 1920 and 1921 the Red Army went into action only against isolated and weak regimes, such as those in the Transcaucasus, which were traditionally part of Tsarist Russia. The operation in Mongolia in 1921 fit into this pattern of very low-risk operations. During the 1920s the Red Army put down the Basmachi Revolt and in the late 1930s fought successful defensive battles against the Japanese army at Lake Khasan and Khalkin-gol. Even in 1939 Stalin was willing to sign the Molotov-Ribbentrop Pact to gain a defensive glacis against Germany and to deflect German troops from the Soviet Union. Thus, there has traditionally been a defensive orientation to Soviet foreign policy, one that has reflected real weakness and has continued into the postwar era.

While this argument is true, it ignores the basic fact that the position of the Soviet Union changed radically after the war. The defensive posture before the war was heavily dictated by the relative weakness of the Soviet Union and, in the 1930s, the growing menace of imperial Japan and Nazi Germany. After World War II these twin dangers had been liquidated and a far more favorable environment in world politics was created to the Soviet Union. This still leaves the question open of why, despite the manifold opportunities open to it after the war, the Soviet Union (as was widely feared, especially by those who compared it with Nazi Germany) did not use its great military power to aggressively advance imperialist goals. The capturing of Eastern Europe was an act approved and supported even by the United States and Great Britain during the course of World War II.

It is in this context that World War II was of great importance. For the postwar world, as was argued in the introductory chapter, was largely shaped by the war and the war, in turn, helped shape Soviet perceptions of the world. Some specific Soviet perceptions that influenced Soviet behavior in certain crises and some more generalizable forms of the impact of the war experience on Soviet foreign policy behavior in major crises will be analyzed in this chapter.

The Soviet World War II experience was especially visible in the crises of 1956, 1961, and 1968 in areas liberated by the Red Army in the course of the war. The Hungarian Revolution, which occurred in a country that witnessed some of the bloodiest battles of the war (the battle for Budapest lasted over four months), was especially troubling to the Soviet leaders. On October 25, 1956, a few days before the intervention, Nikita Khrushchev emotionally told the Yugoslav ambassador to Moscow, Veljko Micunovic, "Anti-Soviet elements have taken up arms against the 'camp' and the Soviet Union. . . . The West is seeking a revision of the results of World War II and has started in Hungary, and will then go on to crush each socialist state in Europe one by one" (Terry 1984: 99). The decision to crush the Hungarian revolt, then, reflected in part the need to retain the World War II patrimony and defensive shield provided by it against possible renewed German aggression or new American imperialism.

Probably in no other crisis was the war experience brought so front and center as in the 1961 Berlin crisis—and for good reason. For the conquest of Berlin came to symbolize not only the great Soviet victories from 1943 to 1945, but also the entire war goal of Stalinist Russia. It was, in short, the apotheosis of the war effort, one gained at the staggering cost of 305,000 casualties in the final battle for Berlin alone. The resolution of the Soviet status came to represent a need felt within the Khrushchevian leadership at the time, as well as a convenient prod to the West to be more responsive to Soviet desires and interests.

To recapitulate all the major references to the war would fill many pages. Several references will suffice to provide the overall picture. When Khrushchev launched his campaign on Berlin in June 1961, he did so on the twentieth anniversary of the invasion of the Soviet Union. Wearing his military uniform of lieutenant general from his days at Stalingrad, Krushchev was flanked by four top Red Army leaders, all with outstanding war records. His speech denounced the aggressive imperialist ambitions of Western leaders who had not fully learned the lessons of the war. Marshal Rodion Malinovsky then blamed the Western powers for starting the war and declared that the Red Army had played a decisive role in the victory. He concluded by arguing that the Western allies had changed neither their methods nor their goals since 1941: "Blinded by class hatred for socialism, they are trying to carry out the same policy that led mankind to World War II" (*Pravda*, 21 June 1961).

Marshal Vasili Chuikov, the hero of Stalingrad, went even further in tying the Berlin campaign to the war by stating that, "the historic truth is that during the assault on Berlin there was not a single American, British or French armed soldier around . . . the claims of the U.S., British and French ruling circles to some kind of special rights in Berlin are entirely unfounded. They did not take it . . . the occupation of Berlin should long since have ended" (*Pravda*, 21 June 1961).

At the end of August 1961, after the erection of the Berlin Wall, a Soviet government statement denouncing the "ever growing aggressiveness of the NATO military bloc" concluded that Soviet war readiness was justified by the fact that "[t]he tragedy of the earliest months of the Great Patriotic War, when Hitler attacked the U.S.S.R. after making sure of his superiority in military equipment, is too fresh in people's minds to allow this to happen today" (Slusser 1973: 161). In early September Khrushchev went even further and portrayed the West German government as madmen itching to repeat the German attack on the Soviet Union. He directly referred to Adenauer, Brandt, and Strauss as "new Hitlers" (Slusser 1973: 196).

Perhaps nowhere was the emotional angst induced by World War II more noticeable than in two speeches by Andrei Gromyko and Nikita Khrushchev. At the Twenty-second Party Congress in October 1961 Gromyko proclaimed,

> The Soviet people is entitled to present West Germany with a bill, which has still by no means been paid in full, for the misfortunes and destruction caused by the Hitlerite invaders on our soil. . . . The Soviet people can without difficulty rouse in themselves a feeling of enmity and anger toward West Germany: they have but to think back on the crimes of the Hitlerite invaders. (Slusser 1973: 419)

And in a remarkable speech at this time Khrushchev indicated that he still saw West Germany, and not the far more powerful United States, as the main enemy. As he asserted,

> "If a third world war is unleashed," Adenauer often said, "West Germany will be the first country to perish." I was pleased to hear this and Adenauer is absolutely right in what he said. For him to be making public statements like that was a great achievement on our part. Not only were we keeping our number one enemy in line, but Adenauer was helping us to keep our other enemies in line too. (Adomeit 1982: 251)

Finally, the Soviet leaders viewed the Prague Spring in 1968 through a distinctly World War II focus. In her study of the crisis Karen Dawisha notes the "omnipresent" nature of the war experience in numerous articles by Soviet marshals recalling the "blood debt" owed by the Czechs to the Red Army for the destruction of the German army in Czechoslovakia during the war. She concludes that in the Soviet Union "leaders and led alike were fixated on the experiences of the Second World War, experiences that led to a universal resolve never again to allow Russia's western borders to be breached" (1984: 347).

The former Red Army commanders from World War II played a notable role in the crisis. As early as May 1968 Marshal Ivan Konev, the former Red Army commander in Prague, began writing a series of articles on the theme that Hitler could have smashed the Prague Uprising but "only the Soviet army had saved Prague" (*Izvestiya*, 5–6 May 1968). Similarly in June 1968 *Krasnaya zvezda*, the army newspaper, carried no less than five articles that stressed that the Czechs should not forget the great Soviet sacrifices in the war (17, 19, 20, 21, 26 July 1968). And, perhaps even more strikingly, in early August 1968 when the Soviet Politburo began to move towards possible approval of the invasion of Czechoslovakia, Sergei Shtemenko replaced M. I. Kazakov as Warsaw Pact chief of staff. The move had ominous overtones as Shtemenko had served as chief of operations in World War II and had directed the liberation of Prague. Even more, he had recently chronicled Stalin's accomplishments in the war, thereby earning the right to direct such a new operation to protect the wartime gains (Dawisha 1984: 271–75).

Zdenek Mylnar, a Czech party secretary who emigrated to the West after 1968, has related several important conversations between the Czech leaders and Leonid Brezhnev. Before the invasion Brezhnev told the Czech leaders

Your country is in the region occupied by Soviet soldiers in World War II. We paid for this with great sacrifices and we will never leave. Your borders are our borders. You do not follow our suggestions and we feel threatened . . . we are completely justified in sending our soldiers to your country in order to be secure within our borders. It is a secondary matter whether or not there is an immediate threat from anyone; this is an issue of principle which will (as it has) remain since World War II.[4]

After the invasion Brezhnev was even more explicit in his conversation with Dubcek after Dubcek had been released from jail. As Mylnar relates,

> Then Brezhnev explained to Dubcek that the end result of all this was Moscow's realization that the Dubcek leadership could not be depended upon . . . Because at this stage matters of the utmost importance were involved: the results of the Second World War. And on those results, Brezhnev was unequivocal: the Second World War had established the borders of socialism at the river Elbe: those borders had been established at great cost to the Soviet people and as a result (Brezhnev direct quote) "the results of the Second World War are inviolable and we will defend them even at the cost of risking a new war."[5]

The General Impact of World War II on Soviet Risk Taking

Clearly, then, the Second World War had a major influence on Soviet foreign policy thinking in the postwar era. But several questions immediately come to the surface. Could not the lessons of World War II be understood in different ways by different leaders? Would not the more dovish leaders in the Kremlin see it as justifying a great stress on peace, given the enormous costs of war? Would not the hawks use it to justify a more aggressive, expansionist policy in light of the irreducible hostility of capitalist imperialist powers? And which parts of the war were important, the earlier or the later phases? And what does World War II have to say in general to the new Soviet generation that lives in a world wholly different economically, politically, and militarily than that of their parents and grandparents almost half a century earlier?

First, the impact of World War II on Soviet perceptions was deeply reinforced by the fact that after 1945 the lessons of Soviet risk taking before 1941 seemed of little relevance. Before 1941 the Soviet Union had existed in a very dangerous world where first international capitalism in the civil war and then the rise of Nazi Germany and imperial Japan in the 1930s had seemed to threaten its very existence. This was a world in which France was thought to have the best army and England the best navy in the world, in which Eastern Europe was dominated by hostile, authoritarian (except for Czechoslovakia) and anti-Soviet governments, in which the United States was a strong but isolationist power. This was a world in which by the late 1930s, with the march of Nazi Germany in the west and border clashes with imperial Japan in the east and the formation of a powerful anti-Comintern alliance, the very existence of the Soviet Union beset by dangerous and powerful enemies seemed to be in doubt. This was a world in which even the Western democratic countries were to acquiesce in the exclusion of the Soviet Union from the vital Munich Conference in 1938 and make no great effort to form a military alliance with Moscow to contain the German expansionism that threatened their very existence. And before 1941 the glory of the British Empire and British power took pride of place before the vast but peacefully slumbering giant in the West, the United States.

After 1945 the relevance of the Soviet prewar conceptions, developed in a world of great danger and little opportunity, seemed to be minimal. By 1945 the menacing anti-Soviet imperialist powers, Nazi Germany and imperial Japan, lay prostrate and occupied by Allied forces. France had been humiliated by the protracted German occupation and, together with England, was well on its way to second-rate status and the loss of its colonial possessions. The once somnolent United States now towered over the rest of the Western world with its economy accounting for almost half of the world's industrial production and its army occupying half of Europe. In this new world the Red Army stood in Berlin, Prague and Vienna and divided a devastated Europe with the American army. By destroying the old order and the old world, the war had created vast new opportunities (and some dangers) for Moscow and altered the very world in which Moscow vied for political and economic standing.

Undeniably, different actors in the Soviet leadership could draw some different lessons from the war, especially in terms of the degree and the extent to which the Soviet Union should cooperate with the West after the war. Some, like Mikhail Gorbachev, have argued that the wartime alliance with the West brought great gains for the Soviet Union and therefore should be continued against new enemies, such as the nuclear threat to the existence of the world. Others, like Andrei Zhdanov and Dmitrii Ustinov, have argued that the war demonstrated the deep hostility of the West to the very existence of the Soviet Union and that, therefore, a posture of eternal vigilance and combativeness is required in the face of an ongoing Western threat to the survival of the country. Furthermore, some bureaucratic actors, such as the military and security police, are more likely to point to instances of Western aggression as demonstrating the need for a hard line posture and a need for the recurrent use of force to ward off Western intrigues while other actors, such as government bureaucrats and economic managers, foreseeing the diversion of important resources, may stress the need for a softer line.

But, this does *not* mean that the war was a procrustean bed from which no meaning could be drawn. Rather there were certain basic lessons on which all could agree and then certain areas in which, as we have already seen, disputes over the lessons of the war were possible. The war, after all, promoted a basic security concensus between Soviet policy leaders from which relatively few Soviet leaders have deviated. Those leaders, such as Beria with regard to East Germany in 1953 and Malenkov with regard to Poland in 1955, who have deviated, have rapidly lost favor and been purged.[6] This is hardly surprising given that the war has been an enormous success in that it has propelled the Soviet Union, as has already been discussed, from a weak and endangered position to one of nascent superpower status in 1945. Indeed, Stalin, although heavily criticized by Nikita Khrushchev and Mikhail Gorbachev for various aspects of his domestic policies, has been largely exempt from criticism in the foreign policy sphere, except for criticism of his lack of preparedness for war in 1941 and his handling of the Yugoslav crisis of 1948.

What, then, did this concensus emerging from World War II emphasize? First, that given the enormous cost of war and its unpredictability peace was a prime necessity for the Soviet Union. The Soviet Union had nearly been destroyed and overrun by Nazi Germany in the first eighteen months of the war. Moscow itself had nearly been taken and territory on which 80 million Russians had lived before 1941 had been occupied during the war by the Germans. The enormous misery of the war, with its staggering military and civilian losses and awesome economic costs, made an enormous impression on Soviet leaders. The Soviet economy had been set back by five to ten years, at least. Furthermore, the confident predictions before the war of a resolute rebuff to any aggressor had proved distressingly wrong after only the first few hours of war.[7] Under these circumstances, the war promoted a deep aversion to any future Soviet participation in a further conflict that could endanger the great gains made by socialism since the October Revolution. Much of the gains made in the 1930s had been destroyed in the war and a future war would probably be more devastating.

This attitude was demonstrated by the extreme reluctance of the Soviet leadership to use force in the postwar era. In the more than four decades since 1945 the Soviet Union, despite a massive and growing military force, has consistently pursued a very cautious and conservative use of force. Moscow has never intervened massively in any conflict, except along its borders, throughout the entire postwar era. When it has encountered any serious risk of escalation from the West, as in the Berlin crises in 1948 and 1961 and the Cuban missile crisis in 1962, it has always backed down. And after Khrushchev's relatively aggressive use of force and bluffs failed, the Brezhnev and Gorbachev regimes, despite much stronger military power, have consistently avoided any confrontations with the West.

Secondly, together with this policy of extreme risk aversion and fear of war, there has been a strong concomitant commitment to the defense of Eastern Europe. For this bordering region was the jumping off point for Operation Barbarossa in 1941, as well as for an earlier German attack in 1915. Retention of Eastern Europe, as Brezhnev indicated in the quotations that appeared earlier in the chapter, was the highest priority for the defense of the Soviet Union. In a hostile world it has provided important security for the fatherland against any possible further attack. Furthermore, Eastern Europe was the great prize of World War II and one that enabled the Soviet Union to make a legitimate claim after 1945 to superpower status. Without Eastern Europe such a claim would have seemed premature and unlikely. In addition, the socialist nature of the region seemed to indicate the validity of the Marxist prediction of the inevitable progress of international socialism. Overall, then, the defense of Eastern Europe became virtually inseparable from that of the Soviet Union.

In this context, therefore, Eastern Europe became the one region in which the Soviet Union has consistently been willing to apply force to maintain the status quo. As before, it has always been willing to make concessions and seek other solutions, as in the case of Poland in 1956 and 1980 or Rumania in the late 1960s. But, when it has felt its "vital interest" threatened and its control slipping in the area, it has never hesitated to pay any international price by the massive use of force, as in Hungary in 1956 and Czechoslovakia in 1968. And even its use of force, from the commanders in charge to the nature of the operation (massive in scope and rapid in execution), have borne the trademarks of the war experience. The 1979 invasion of bordering Afghanistan was quite similar in many characteristics.[8]

Thirdly, the war experience had a distinctive impact on the Soviet evaluation of risk taking. It promoted a very conservative evaluation of risk, given the serious divergence between Soviet expectations and realities. The 1941 Stalinist expectation of a viable Red Army defense and the near disaster at the hands of the Wehrmacht promoted this view. So, too, did the overextension of the Red Army in its early counteroffensives of 1941 and 1942. Furthermore, the great stocks of military supplies and large potentially mobilizable military manpower of 1941 failed to protect the Soviet Union in 1941. Thus, this promoted the need the Soviet felt for massive military overinsurance and preparation against any possible contingency. So, too, did the extreme cost and protracted duration of time before final victory was achieved in 1945.

In turn, this meant that worst-case scenarios could never be ignored, for they had come true in World War II. Only in the worst nightmare of a Soviet war planner would the actual course of events of 1941 and 1942 have seemed possible. This meant, of course, that there was a need for a very strongly positive benefit-cost ratio and careful evaluation of all enemy potential before any military intervention could be approved in the postwar world. This also reinforced the Leninist dictum of despising the enemy tactically but respecting him strategically. Overall, then, these military considerations reinforced the first two tendencies stressed above: the need to avoid war except when absolutely necessary and the need to prevent Eastern Europe from becoming a dangerous launching ground for new reckless Western assaults on the Soviet Union.

Fourthly, the war promoted an obsession with the danger posed by Germany to Soviet survival. The deep hatred and fear of West Germany and the extremely tight rein held by Moscow in East Germany in the postwar period certainly exceeded any "rational" considerations. Stalin's well-known statement after the war that in another fifteen to twenty years the Soviet Union would "have another go" with Germany fit into this category well (Djilas 1962: 114–15). So, too, did Khrushchev's obsession with Berlin and the importance the Kremlin placed on better relations with West Germany during the Brezhnev years. Despite the enormous asymmetry in power between the two sides in the postwar era, West Germany, and not simply in terms of propaganda, retained a powerful image as the ultimate enemy of the Soviet Union. Only after the success of *Ostpolitik* in the 1970s did China finally displace West Germany as the main enemy. This obsession was to play a significant role, for example, in the 1948 and 1961 Berlin crises and in the 1968 Czechoslovakia crisis when Moscow feared a new emerging Bonn-Prague axis.

Finally, there were images of the West from the war that remained indelibly etched in the minds of the Soviet leaders. Two principal images remained after the war. One was of great Western power, and especially American power, demonstrated during the war. Soviet leaders were impressed by the relative ease with which the Anglo-American forces smashed German forces in France and Germany in the final year of the war, the massive Allied strategic bombing campaign that reduced much of Germany to rubble, and the dropping of two American atomic bombs on Hiroshima and Nagasaki. They could not but be awed by the thorough destruction and occupation of imperial Japan, the overpowering American naval power that turned the Atlantic and Pacific oceans into American preserves, and the huge Lend Lease program of shipments (11 billion dollars in total) to the Soviet Union. They witnessed the vast cornucopia of goods, both civilian and military, that were turned out during the war by an American economy four times greater than theirs. All this, especially in combination with the American allies in Western Europe, promoted a deep desire to avoid any confrontation with such a powerful enemy and ensured a deep respect for Western capabilities.

At the same time, though, there was a second image of the West fostered by the events of the prewar and war years. This was the image of the deep hostility of the Western capitalist powers to the Soviet Union and its very existence. From the Soviet perspective, the Western capitalist powers had done very little to aid the Soviet Union in resisting German and Japanese imperialism during the 1930s. Through appeasement at Munich the Western capitalist powers had often aided and abetted the enemies of the Soviet Union. They had scorned all Soviet attempts to build a serious antifascist alliance with the Western allies. This unreliability of the Western countries to oppose fascism was paralleled by the inability of the Western working class to mount a serious challenge to fascism.

From the Soviet perspective, during the war the Western countries did relatively little to oppose Nazi Germany until the final year of the war. From June 1941 until June 1944 over 6 million soldiers in the Red Army died and 5 million were taken prisoner—while the losses of Britain and the United States numbered less than 200,000 men. While the Western allies were leisurely fighting small-scale actions against, at best, 10–20 German divisions on the periphery of the Third Reich in North Africa, Sicily and Italy, the Soviet Union was regularly confronting 150–200 German divisions on the Eastern front. And only when the Red Army had largely expelled the German invaders from Soviet territory at enormous cost did the Allies finally launch the often promised but never delivered second front in 1944 to prevent the Red Army from occupying the entire European continent. Even then, in the final year of the war, the Red Army did the bulk of the fighting as over 1 million soldiers died compared to 200,000 for the British and American armies.[9]

Furthermore, the Soviet leaders felt the war demonstrated the true duplicity of the Allied leaders. After all, in their view the West was enormously powerful and capable. How, then, could one explain the marked incapacity of the West to launch any meaningful second front to draw off significant numbers of German troops to the West from the Eastern front—a neglect that lasted from 1941 until 1944, a time when the very future of the Soviet Union was at stake? This was especially true given the Western promises to open such a front both in 1942 and 1943 and then the reality of small-scale Western actions in North Africa and Sicily and Italy. The enormous gap between Western economic power and its military power projection could only cause grave concern in the Kremlin during the war.

This was made even more manifest during the final months of the war in 1945 by the relative ease of the advance of the Anglo-American forces in the West compared to the extremely difficult resistance encountered in the East by the Red Army in East Prussia,

Hungary and around Berlin. All this reinforced a deep and profound hostility towards the Western powers, even more so when after the war those powers denigrated Soviet military accomplishments and exaggerated their own (Stoler 1977).

The impact, then, of the war was to greatly reinforce the traditional prewar Soviet and essentially Marxist views of the capitalist states. These views played a direct role in the development of the cold war and the need to guard the Eastern European glacis in particular and the border areas in general against Western penetration. This need was further heightened by the Western opposition to granting recognition of the Soviet control of the region after the war and Soviet control for democratic elections. This Western desire was seen as absurd, since none of these countries, except for Czechoslovakia, had been democratic in the interwar period, and dangerous, given the largely anti-Soviet nature of the populace. In short, the Western unwillingness to acknowledge the basic Soviet perception of its role in World War II played a major role in reinforcing the importance of those lessons in the minds of Soviet leaders.

World War II, then, played a major role in shaping Soviet perceptions and actions after the war. The war promoted a very cautious approach to risk taking, a desire to use force only in the border areas and primarily in Eastern Europe, and even then only with a very positive evaluation of the benefits and costs of such an operation. There was a strong desire to avoid any possible confrontation with the West and the need for large-scale military overinsurance in any case. All these lessons reinforced the basic conservative, prewar Soviet foreign policy, even in a new situation in which many in the West feared that the nascent superpower would use its military superiority in land power in Europe and Asia for military expansionism on the Nazi model. These fears have proved to be groundless, as the Soviet Union has used military power more cautiously than has the United States in the postwar era.

The new Gorbachev regime seems determined to go even further in this direction than its predecessors. It is committed to lessening the dangers of war with the West through arms control agreements with the West, as seen in the INF accord reached at the Washington summit in December 1987. Along its borders it is trying to pull its troops out of Afghanistan, improve relations with the People's Republic of China, and create a more stable relationship with its Eastern European clients. Given the instability in Eastern Europe that has accompanied previous reform periods in the Soviet Union under Khrushchev and the early years of the Brezhnev regime, the road ahead is likely to be difficult. The nationality rioting in Armenia and Azerbaijan in February and March 1988 may presage future problems in Eastern Europe as well. But, the fundamental legacy of World War II will ensure that any Soviet leadership, reformist or conservative, will continue to apply the basic rules of the security concensus greatly reinforced by those far off, bloody and decisive events that transpired from June 1941 until May 1945 on the battlefields of Europe.

Notes

1 For the bureaucratic politics model, see Slusser 1973 and Valenta 1979, as well as Rice and Fry in Adelman 1986: 181–99. For a more uniform view, see Adomeit 1982 and Dawisha 1984.

2 As Michael Brecher has analyzed the Herculean task facing any scholar in this field,

    To dissect Soviet decision making and behavior in foreign policy crises requires diverse skills: A knowledge of the language, the history and the political system and ideology of the USSR, as well as insight into the personality traits and interpersonal relations of Soviet leaders; an ability to apply psychology findings on the dynamics of small group behavior to the pivotal group at the apex of the Soviet power pyramid, the Politburo; a familiarity with the methods of modern social science and a disposition to combine rigorous, systematic inquiry with foreign area specialization; a mastery of the available source materials, written and oral, which are indispensable for an in-depth case study; a capacity to assemble the evidence from a myriad of sources, much of it open to conflicting interpretation, and to relate such data to basic questions about the decision-making process; and finally, a talent for clarifying the often blurred features of Soviet behavior.

    See Dawisha 1984: ix.

3 For Berlin 1948 see Adomeit 1982. For Berlin 1961 see Adomeit 1982 and Slusser 1973. For Hungary 1956 see Gati 1986 and Rice and Fry in Adelman 1986: 181–99. For Poland 1980 see Ploss 1986 and Wozniuk 1987. For Czechoslovakia 1968 see Valenta 1979 and Dawisha 1984.

4 Zdenek Mylnar quoted in Dawisha 1984: 256.

5 Zdenek Mylnar quoted in Dawisha 1984: 331.

6 For Beria see Brzezinski 1961: 155 and for Malenkov see Mastny 1978: 37–51.

7 For good material on the nature of the war, see Linz 1985.

8 See Gibson in Adelman 1986: 266–85.

9 For the statistics and the general argument, see the book by Adelman 1988.

5

Preparing for War: Economic and Military Mobilization Past and Present

Cristann Lea Gibson

In the years since the end of World War II, few topics have dominated the discussions of the war and the lessons to be learned for contemporary Soviet planners more than the issue of mobilization has. Although the necessity for timing and the risks of mobilization have changed as debates over the type of future wars and their origins have evolved, no other wartime experience has so completely determined the changes in military strategy that came afterward.

The phases of the economic and military mobilizations that occurred with the outbreak of hostilities between the Soviet Union and Germany in June of 1941 left an enduring record of positive and negative lessons regarding the timing, methods, and goals of preparedness. The experience also unleashed an ongoing debate about the connections between preparedness, risk, and the beginning period of war. Whether planners were being asked to base their assumptions on another world war that involved total, open mobilization or a partial, concealed mobilization, such as those undertaken in Czechoslovakia, Afghanistan and later Poland, Soviet planning and implementation was largely based on what had been learned during the Great Patriotic War.

Wartime experience had shown that without a well-developed and readily convertible production base in the defense sector prior to the outbreak of war the mobilized forces would be unable to recover from initial losses. The Soviets admit, however, that no modern nation can maintain a fully mobilized war economy and a fully mobilized force in peacetime. Therefore postwar efforts have concentrated on building up the peacetime defense base of the nation by making it more efficient, productive, secure and convertible.

With regard to the mobilization of the armed forces, the Second World War showed that success in war was contingent upon a preplanned and well arranged registration and training of the draftable population (Universal Military Training, or UMT), the organized notification and assembly of reservists in combat-ready units, the simultaneous mobilization of the means of transportation, the peacetime stockpiling of necessary stores of weapons, military equipment and supplies in mobile decentralized locations, and the prompt strategic deployment of the armed forces in forward areas. In addition, military strategy had to encompass defensive as well as offensive missions in order to be responsive to the form and dynamic of modern warfare. Most of all the war taught the Soviets the value of correctly and rapidly ascertaining the capabilities and intentions of the enemy and preparing themselves to wage war without a prolonged period of peacetime mobilization. The Soviet Union survived in the face of incredible odds due to the successful and timely mobilization of the total economic and military might of the nation. The fact that despite terrible losses of men, resources, and territory during the initial period of the war the Soviets were able to convert industry and mobilize and deploy an enormous force is never far from the minds of contemporary Soviet planners. In this way the wartime experience has shaped the postwar debates concerning the overall issues of mobilization in terms of preparedness, combat readiness, and the beginning period of war.

This chapter will look at the Soviet mobilization experience from several standpoints. The first will be the issue of whether or not the Soviets should mobilize. According to the lessons the Soviets have learned from their disparate experiences during World War I and World War II, does preparedness and especially mobilization heighten the risk of war, or does the possibility of repeating the losses suffered in the initial period of the Great Patriotic War due to remaining unprepared in the face of hostilities pose the greatest and most untenable risk?

The next aspect of mobilization that will be addressed is the actual experience of the economic and military mobilizations during the Great Patriotic War. Without a thorough understanding of the methods and outcomes of this experience the reasons behind contemporary Soviet analysis and planning for mobilization are difficult to assess.

Finally, I will look at mobilization planning as it exists today. The successes and failures of mobilization during the war have led directly to the present methods and goals of Soviet planners. In addition mobilization during the war has shaped the political and military responsibilities of the professional military with regard to modern warfare. In this sense, it is important to know how mobilization is defined and planned in light of the past, because ultimately mobilization is a window to the vision of future wars and the way in which they will be fought.

Mobilization in Two Wars: Preparedness versus Caution

The Soviet experience with total, open, economic and military mobilization is based on two diverse examples, World War I and World War II. In 1914, because of a period of prolonged diplomatic maneuvering, preparations for war were set into motion long before hostilities began. Mobilization of the main forces and their forward deployment was largely achieved during a period of minor border engagements or outright standoffs. The majority of the forces were massed long before any serious engagement with the enemy occurred. Aside from typical shortages of equipment and transport there was no disruption in achieving full military mobilization and economic conversion. Therefore, the prolonged mobilization period of World War I ultimately had little effect on the subsequent course of the war.

Of the many lessons the World War I mobilization experience imparted to policymakers and military planners, a deadly combination of caution regarding preparedness as a path to war and confidence in the offensive nature of future war guaranteed a radically different mobilization experience in World War II. World

War I had taught the Soviets that the nature of preparations in the face of possible conflict and the consequences of a series of misperceptions and provocative responses, in effect, made going to war almost certain once mobilization reached a certain level. Strategically, World War I served as a primer on caution over preparedness. Combined with this general perception was the persistent view, despite growing evidence to the contrary, that the beginning period of the next war would wait while mobilization proceeded.[1] The military planner's strategy of offensive engagements was dependent on the majority of the economic and military mobilization and deployment being completed prior to the outbreak of full-blown hostilities.

On June 22, 1941, when Nazi Germany invaded the Soviet Union with a premobilized force comprising the majority of their combat-ready blitzkrieg troops, the Soviets were totally unprepared. Despite discrete troop movements (Khorkov 1986: 10–11) and long-term economic preparations,[2] the lack of any real mobilization immediately placed the Soviets at an impossible economic and military disadvantage and left them to learn defensive operations on the run. In the first days of the war the German army moved great distances, claiming the offensive in very rapid campaigns. Before the Soviets could recover from the loss of their agricultural and industrial heartland, the total disruption of economic conversion, supply and transport and begin to mobilize men and material according to almost obsolete plans, the Germans had taught them a lesson regarding the beginning period of war that would persist to the present day. Delaying mobilization or being unprepared to wage war may critically effect the entire course of the war and inflict insurmountable damage to a nation's security. In this sense preparedness ultimately took on a much greater value, as it became synonymous with survival.

The experiences of the initial period of World War II were not fully internalized as a part of military doctrine until after the death of Stalin in 1953.[3] The failure to adequately prepare and mobilize for war in the first months of the summer of 1941 was ascribed in part to the element of strategic surprise, or, in more recent accounts, to the willing disregard by Stalin and his advisors of the obvious preparations and signals of an impending confrontation. Stalin's denial of the mounting German threat, combined with his sustained effort to avoid antagonizing Hitler, effectively prevented the Soviets from openly mobilizing and deploying sufficient forces to counter the Nazi invasion.[4] As an article in the Soviet General Staff journal *Military Thought* stated, "The lack of a timely decision to bring the Soviet troops to combat readiness and occupy proper regions and boundaries near the state borders had extremely bad consequences for us and essentially predetermined the major setbacks and defeats of the Soviet army in the beginning period of war (Biryuzov 1964: 12).

Although industry was specifically oriented toward defense concerns from 1938 to 1941, the evacuation of industry and its conversion to a war footing did not take place until the war actually began. By the time industry responded to the realities of the war much had been lost to the enemy both in raw materials and industrial capacity.

In light of the post-war analysis of the initial period of World War II in the 1950s and early 1960s, an overriding conclusion was reached by Soviet political and military leaders regarding preparedness. If the possibility exists that despite prudent responses you may have to fight, you should prepare for that outcome regardless of the political costs. In starker terms, if the conflict appears to be inevitable it is better to have the capability to strike first from a fully prepared posture.

The move to preemption as an extension of strategic surprise added a more deadly aspect to the experience of World War II. The Soviets could not readily accept a situation or policy that put them in the position to take the first blow or remain mutually vulnerable. The goal of preserving the element of timeliness in warfare would necessitate preemption in the face of sufficient probable cause on the part of an enemy. Because preparedness at any cost with the ultimate value placed on timeliness is a particularly insensitive model of behavior during crisis situations, strategically it involves a high degree of risk. It is a military position that always assumes and prepares for the worst case, taking mobilization measures that, in effect, ignore signaling and opposing responses in order to assure the combat capability and survivability of the Soviet force.

As Soviet security concerns in the 1960s and 1970s lead to the rise of arms control initiatives, the necessities of maintaining detente demanded that the Soviet policy of preparedness at any cost become more conscious of the realities of crisis and provocation. Although

Brezhnev and the political leadership were acutely aware of the necessity for "waging peace" (*Pravda*, 3 January and 16 March 1974) military leaders, among them chief of the General Staff V. Kulikov and Defense Minister Grechko, continued to voice the position that military preparedness and timeliness were the best way of preventing war (*Pravda*, 13 November 1974; *Krasnaya zvezda* 19 March 1974). Despite the ebb and flow of detente and arms control in subsequent years, Soviet military leaders have been fairly consistent on this theme. Recently, in many military journals the failure to mobilize in a timely fashion and to an adequate degree in 1941 is undergoing still another revival (Khorkov 1986: 9–15; Lushev 1987:3–14). These articles once again state the military view that only advance preparedness is both a deterrent and a form of insurance.

At the same time the strategic leadership during the 1970s and into the 1980s has remained acutely aware that initiating preventative military activity even in the form of premobilization may make going to war a certainty. Although it is true that the political leaders are aware of the military problems that are involved in choosing caution in the face of crisis, it is also true that only the political leaders determine policy. As Brezhnev said in 1974, "the military decide what to shoot at, while the political leadership decides whether or not to shoot."[5]

The two past models of Soviet behavior with regard to mobilization present totally opposite experiences that counsel exclusive policies. From a military point of view the costs of remaining unprepared are untenable and from the political side the costs of provoking war through mobilization and counter-mobilization are very real. Since there is no simple solution to these issues, in future periods of crisis the extent and timing of Soviet mobilization and deployment may, however, reveal the type of confrontation they expect to pursue and the degree to which they are committed to it.[6] It cannot be reasonably argued that the Soviets are not aware of the risks inherent in mobilizing since they admit that even partial mobilization cannot be reliably obscured in the present-day conditions of sensitive reconnaissance. Even mobilizing men and material in gradual stages or under the cover of conducting military exercises and long-term maneuvers cannot be disguised.

Military and Economic Mobilization: The Great Patriotic War

As the Soviet economy began to recover with the First Five-Year Plan (1928–32) the defense industries received increasing priority. The Second Five-Year Plan (1933–37) specifically addressed the need to create new bases of industry in the east (to reduce the mobilization deployment) and to update technology. In 1934 defense budgets began to expand relative to the total budget (U.S. Department of State 1945: 6). By 1936 the percentage of the GNP allocated for defense was 18.8 percent.

Beginning with the Third Five-Year Plan (1938–42) primary attention was paid to strengthening and expanding the defense industries by expanding the fuel and power base, further modernizing and developing metallurgy (especially high-quality metallurgy), and developing precision machine building. Due in part to these measures, from 1938 to the beginning of the war in 1941 the percentage of GNP devoted to military industry had continued to rise from 27.5 percent to 42.6 percent.[7] As a result of the concentration on defense in the few years before the war the increase in the gross output of the defense industries occurred considerably faster than that of all of the other industries.

During the prewar years Stalin paid particular attention to expanding all branches of defense production—artillery, aviation, the tank industry and military ship building, along with general industrial production that would help with the development and eventual conversion of the military industries. Specialized scientific research institutes, major military design bureaus and experimental productions at military enterprises were created to begin the development and production of new equipment and weapons. As a result, during the prewar period aviation, artillery systems, mortars, the M-1891-1930 Mosin rifle, automatic small arms weapons, and the SHSG Shpagin submachine gun were improved, and the new types that were made were produced with virtually no improvements during the war.[8]

During the prewar period the primary "mobilization task" was qualitatively and rapidly rebuilding industry in terms of production processes and capacities in order to produce new combat equipment. This involved the expansion of the production and technical resource base of the armament industry. Old plants were renovated and expanded and new ones were built in the Urals, the

Volga, eastern and western Siberia, Central Asia and the Far East.[9] Young cadres of armament workers were trained, specialists were diverted to the defense industries, skilled workers were trained through a plant training network, and extensive industrial reserves of special equipment, raw materials and skilled manpower were created and stockpiled.[10] The concentrated efforts to standardize and simplify manufacturing methods, maximize plant specialization, and maximize duplication in the production of the most important weapons (machine building and training along with component manufacture) meant that by the eve of the war the armaments industry was in a better qualitative and quantitative position to wage war. Despite all of the prewar efforts, however, there was a slowdown in overall industrial production. This was due to the rapid pace of the reorganization and modernization of industry and to the massive conversion of machinery and other industrial plants to armament production (Schwartz 1968).

In 1940, after the Russo-Finnish war, the Supreme Soviet approved an additional large increase in defense expenditures. On June 26 the Presidium of the Supreme Soviet placed Soviet industry virtually on a war footing. The eight-hour day, six-day work week was instituted and no migration of labor was allowed. By January of 1941 labor discipline became even more rigorously enforced with severe penalties for absenteeism (Werth 1964: 90). All prewar planning was based on the assumption that the war with Germany would begin sometime in 1942, so although a great deal had been accomplished by June of 1941, the invasion still caught industry unprepared for the mass mobilization that would be necessary.

With the beginning of the war on 22 June 1941 and the rapid loss of the most significant economic regions of the country industrial capacity immediately declined by 38 percent. By November of 1941 overall industrial capacity had declined by 47 percent due to losses and conversion (Vannikov 1968–69: 118). The survival of the Soviet Union depended upon the mass mobilization of manpower and war industries within the unoccupied territories.

The territories subjected to German occupation were populated by over 70 million people, roughly 40 percent of the prewar population, and comprised most of the agricultural and industrial base of the nation. In addition the main machine building areas were in Moscow, Leningrad and Tula—which were in the area of military operations. Major sources of raw materials, metals and petroleum had been overrun by the Germans by the end of 1941.[11] The one saving factor was that most of the production of ordnance for the ground force artillery was located in the deep rear (Vannikov 1968–69: 121).

The Soviet ability to continue to wage war was entirely dependent upon the rapid relocation of industry or the building of new production centers in the east, on the Volga, in the Urals, in Central Asia or in western Siberia, the location and development of new resource areas, the massive reequipment of the Red Army, the recruitment and training of labor (from 14 years of age and including both sexes), the extension of the work week to seven days and twenty-four-hour shifts, and the forced conservation of skilled labor and materials. All energies of the population were directed toward regaining productive capacity and supplying the front.

The major administrative and policy-making body that controlled all war-related actions was the State Defense Committee (GKO). This committee was formed on June 30, 1941 by a joint decision of the Central Committee of the CPSU, the Presidium of the Supreme Soviet, and the Council of the People's Commissars of the USSR, "in order to coordinate the activities of all State institutions, Party, Komsomol and trade union organizations," and to deal with "all state security and public orders" (*Pravda* 30 June 1941: 1). The GKO controlled all national economic activity of the country, determined the direction and volume of military industry, distributed manpower and material resources between the front and the rear, and decided problems of foreign policy and diplomatic practice (Lomov 1966: 1–2).

As a command structure the GKO had the force of martial law behind its decrees and it could readily supercede any other government or party command. The GKO relied heavily on the Council of People's Commissars and the Urban Defense Committees for planning and implementing both on the state and local level. They were directly responsible for organizing citizen defense, raising a militia, taking over localized industry, rationing food and other goods, and controlling supply. In this amalgamation of political and administrative power they were assisted by representatives of the Red Army, the People's Commissariat of Internal Affairs (NKVD) and the party. The first secretaries of *oblasts* and *riaons* were the representatives of the GKO in local areas (Pospelov 1974: 77–78).

Stalin was appointed chairman of the committee and all eight members were also members or alternates to the Politburo. Of the members, Malenkov, Beria, and Kaganovich were directly concerned with industrial construction and expansion of heavy industry, especially in the production of tanks, aircraft, armaments and munitions. Imports of vital commodities and the military supply of fuel, food and clothing were under the supervision of Mikoyan. Voznesenskii, chairman of the Supreme Economic Council and the State Planning Commission, was directly responsible for evacuating industry. Voroshilov, as the former People's Commissar of Defense, provided all liaison and coordinating functions with the Supreme High Command of the Armed Forces (STAVKA). The direct link to the Council of People's Commissars was Molotov, who was a former chairman of the council. Through this body reservists were mobilized and trained, resources were redistributed to supply the armed forces and industry was converted to a war footing.

On June 30 a mobilization plan for converting the national economy was approved by the GKO for the third quarter of 1941. As an article on the conversion stated, "plants producing military equipment, weapons and ammunition, power plants, metallurgy, mechanical and oil refining production and railroads were declared to be shock projects" (Ivashov 1987: 39). During the first summer of the war the immediate concerns were to convert plants producing heavy transport and agricultural machinery to tank production while converting medium machine building plants to the production of artillery and mortars. In order to accomplish all this, between July of 1941 and January of 1942, the Committee for the Registration and Allocation of the Labor Force was able to mobilize from local industries, industrial cooperatives and the various municipal economies, 120,830 people. From unemployed labor—children, housewives, and seniors—an additional 860,000 people were mobilized for industrial conversion by the second half of 1942.[12]

In overall terms the very production of weaponry was changed during the period of reorganization. Weapons systems were simplified, and models were discontinued that demanded the import of raw materials or extensive retooling. Local resources and materials were used extensively to cut down on transport time and vulnerability. In essence this small level of autonomy in effect reduced the risk to, or importance of, any one region or plant.

During the summer and fall of 1941 military output decreased due to the massive industrial evacuation to the east.[13] By December 1941 the decline was stopped and there was a gradual upsurge as transport and conversion problems were corrected. From March of 1942 the volume of industrial production began to grow rapidly but it was not until June of 1942 that the August 1941 level of output was reached and the conversion of the economy was completed (Vannikov 1968–69: 119).

Without the long-term modernization and rebuilding of the Soviet economy before the war and the vast amount of resources and manpower allotted to the defense industries the Soviets could not have withstood the losses of the first months of the war. The fact that industry was able to complete the transition to a totally mobilized state despite occupation and the disruption of supply, raw materials, equipment and transport is still one of the great achievements of the Second World War.

Ultimately the mobilization and survival of the Red Army depended upon the economic mobilization of the Soviet state. The linkage between these two components of the mobilization process, so completely demonstrated during the war, continues to be a major factor concerning contemporary military planners.

At the same time the economy was being prepared for war the armed forces were undergoing a much slower and more disruptive series of preparations. Starting with the Second Five-Year Plan (1933–37) the overall concentration was on the "technical reconstruction and rearming of the troops with modern combat equipment" (Khorkov 1987: 15). During the same period the emphasis was also on the increase in troop strength. As a result the number of men under arms rose from 885,000 in 1933 to 1,513,400 in 1938, with 77 percent of all rifle divisions becoming regular.[14]

The Third Five-Year Plan (1938–42) further specified the "augmentation and deployment of the ground troops, artillery of the Reserve High Command (RGK) and the air and naval forces as well as the further establishment of large armored formations" (Khorkov 1987: 15). In order to secure this larger, more modern force, a decree of the Council of People's Commissars dated July 7, 1938 created independent military commissariats (*Voyenkomat*) in all autonomous republics, *krays*, *oblasts*, national districts, autonomous oblasts and cities and at the same time it increased the network of *rayon* military commissariats.[15]

The military commissariats were responsible for mobilization, conducting call-ups, calculation of resource manpower, categorization and regulation, reserve training, staffing newly created units with command cadres, and sending new cadets to military schools. Along with the Komsomol (All-Union Leninist Communist League of Youth) and the Voluntary Society for Cooperation with the Armed Forces (DOSAFF), they assisted schools, technicums, universities, sports camps, *kolhozes* and industrial plants with predraft training for military induction. To augment basic training the network of military training institutes was also expanded so that by early 1941 they had more than doubled.

Although some form of UMT had been in effect since the mid-1920s, the system was reformed on September 1, 1939 with the adoption of the Law on Universal Military obligation. This law "permitted an increase in the personnel strength of the Armed Forces in the years 1939–41 by almost threefold, the formation of 125 new divisions and an increase in the combat readiness of the Red Army" (Grechko 1975: 47). Induction was then done by unit (usually battalion) rather than individual call-up. Since all Soviet citizens were subject to military service unless specifically excluded, service and technical personnel were easily acquired. In addition, entire administrations (signal communications, transportation) were militarized by decree. Preinvasion mobilization increased the strength of the armed forces from 1,513,400 men in 1938 to 4,207,000 in January of 1941.[16]

By March of 1941, although Stalin had called up additional reserves, of the total 303 infantry, tank, motorized and cavalry divisions in all military districts only 125 were combat ready. Others were still critically short of equipment, weapons, training, transport and command.[17] In addition, most of the rear service entities were not fully deployed since according to the mobilization plan, *tyl* (rear) units would be attached to individual divisions as they were called up.

Part of the severe shortage of equipment, weapons and ammunition, despite the growth of defense production, was due to the significant changes that had occurred in the organization and establishment of various elements of the central command apparatus, the field forces, formations and units of the armed forces from 1939 to 1941. Rifle formations increased, more mechanized corps (29) were created by absorbing the tank battalions of infantry divisions and individual tank brigades, and the total number of air regiments nearly doubled. This rapid growth in size and type of forces also limited the combat capabilities of the individual units and created a shortage of command personnel. Command problems were also made more severe because of the loss of combat experienced senior and midlevel officers due to the 1937–38 purges.

As tensions with Germany heightened in the spring of 1941, forward deployment began as troops were moved from the interior to strategic sectors. About half of the entire force was located in the Leningrad, Baltic Special, Western Special, Kiev Special and Odessa military districts and the corresponding fleets. These troops were relocated secretly in incremental movements under the guise of sending the units to camps (Khorkov 1986: 12). These movements also caused additional problems for the newly formed forces. Most of the troops were stationed in new regions with inadequate fortifications, housing, supply lines, storage and transport facilities. These new formations were not fully manned and were without engagement orders.[18] The General Staff had assumed these troops would be brought to a full state of readiness within the first days of mobilization. As one source on the war so succinctly states, "The whole defense of the State frontier was based on the assumption that a surprise attack by the Germans was out of the question."[19] These partially manned, equipped and trained forces were the troops that would take the brunt of the German attack and as they were overrun they virtually dissolved.

With the German invasion on June 22, 1941 a state of martial law was declared in the western districts and on the next day mobilization began on a mass scale with the call-up of reservists born from 1905 to 1918. In the western districts a state of near chaos developed when mobilization contingents were sent from assembly points, according to plans, to the supposed location of military units only to find these points were often abandoned by the retreating army. As a result many draftees and whole units were momentarily lost and replacement of personnel was all but impossible. The plan for troop movements based on highly centralized orders from other military districts also met with disrupted communication, overrun positions, and snarled transport. The troops in the Baltic, Kiev and western military districts were left with insurmountable shortages that impaired their ability to fight.

In the remaining districts mobilization proceeded according to the prewar plans, unhindered by the enemy advance. As a result, in the first eight days of the war 5.3 million people were mobilized by activating reserve units.[20] Military formations were mobilized in every republic, *oblast* and *kray* and totalled 291 divisions and 94 brigades by December of 1941.[21]

Initially the most difficult problems for mobilized forces were transport and supply. This was exacerbated by a system of decentralized control that was finally reorganized under the centralized control of the rear services in late July. The immediate problem was the replenishment of the stationary supply depots and stockpiles of equipment that had fallen to the Germans in the first days of the war. As a result of these shortages and the disruption of defense production and transport during the first months of the war, many tank and mechanized units fought without needed tanks, artillery and combat equipment.

With an additional call-up in August it was possible to form new units while strengthening those that already were deployed, and replacing the losses at the front. By December 1941 the Soviet armed forces had fielded eight operational fronts and four separate armies.[22]

Despite the total mobilization of the summer and fall of 1941 these months were a disaster for the Soviet forces. The greater part of the air force was wiped out in the first days of the war because most of the air units were concentrated at airfields without camouflage or adequate air defenses. They were deployed close to the frontier while others were being built or reconstructed. The Soviets lost thousands of tanks and hundreds of thousands of soldiers were captured.

The staggering losses in the initial period of the war can be directly attributed to a disastrous combination of factors that comprise the major lessons of the Great Patriotic War: the failure to mobilize and deploy forces in combat condition and strength prior to massed engagements, inadequate training, supply and transport, the unrealistic assessment of the force's combat capability, the lack of defensive strategy, and the underestimation of the enemy.

Mobilization for Future War

In the years since World War II Soviet military planners have been concerned with the interrelated issues of preparedness, mobilization, and the beginning period of war and have focused their analyses on the failures and successes of the wartime mobilization experience. Although contemporary planners have differed over time as to the importance of such issues as surprise, the duration of the conventional phase of a future war, and the effect of nuclear weapons on mobilization, they agree that the long-term issue of the overall level of economic and military preparedness prior to the actual outbreak of hostilities is critical in modern warfare. In this sense, the military industrial base, the level of forces, their combat readiness and deployment at the start of the war will be the primary determinants of the outcome, not only of the initial period of war, but of the entire course of the war.

The possibility of a nuclear phase in a future war does not automatically lessen the importance of mobilization. Soviet planners from the mid-1970s have envisioned a future war consisting of either a prolonged conventional phase as a part of a protracted war or beginning with some indefinite period of crisis during which some form of mobilization would take place.[23] Therefore as one military planner has observed, "It is impossible to escape a certain period of conversion from peacetime to wartime . . . the problem of mobilization remains an indispensible category of war" (Korniyenko 1968: 9).

The Great Patriotic War demonstrated that military preparedness (mobilization, combat readiness) and the ability to continue to conduct the war was entirely dependent upon the level of economic preparedness. Given the nature of modern warfare the necessity for developing a strong defense production base during peacetime is essential to the ability to wage war. Since extensively expanding military industries once the war has begun is virtually impossible, the basic level of the peacetime production and reserves (manpower as well as emergency, mobilization and strategic reserves) of the regular defense industries actually determines the overall military capability of the nation (Korniyenko 1968: 9). Once hostilities begin only those industries already in production and those immediately convertible will be useful.

The success of present day economic mobilization, therefore, depends on measures taken in peacetime to build up the defense base and allows a minimal and rapid conversion of industry to a war footing. This involves improving the overall mechanical and technological basis of industrial production in order to modernize heavy industry, the military assembly industry (manufacture of machinery, assemblies and finished products), and the military production industry (manufacture of finished goods) (Cherednichenko 1971: 22).

Since the possible use of nuclear weapons and the rapid pace and wide range of operations in modern warfare make the evacuation of industry virtually impossible, the ability to preserve the viability of the industrial base is ensured in postwar planning by the territorial dispersion of enterprises and reserves, and the duplication of production. In this way economic regions rely on the cooperation of production within individual regions in order to eliminate the transportation of individual parts, assemblies, half-finished products, fuel, and raw materials. Standardization of supplies for the armed forces and the standardization of the production of military and civilian equipment has also cut down on conversion time and eliminated the need for stockpiling equipment that can rapidly obsolesce (Sokolovskii 1975: 322–23).

Despite these measures, in any war that involves a nuclear operations phase or a long conventional phase the most vulnerable points for timely economic conversion, and the maintenance and deployment of production output are the same as they were during the previous war—agriculture, transportation and reserves of skilled manpower and raw materials. Even in the partial mobilizations in 1968 (Czechoslovakia), 1979 (Afghanistan) and in 1980 (the aborted intervention in Poland) these problems were readily apparent. On a larger scale than these operations or with the permanent disruption of any or all of these factors the continuation of defense production would be all but impossible.

Military preparedness, in contemporary terms, is based on the combat readiness of the forces, their mobilization, and their timely deployment prior to the beginning period of war. While the economy can be developed in the long term to mask the mobilization level and capacity of the defense industries, and combat readiness can also be primarily accomplished in the long term, mobilization of men and material is a direct measure that is both more provocative, and more difficult to mask under present conditions (Garayev 1985: 241–43).

Although Soviet planners specify that mobilization can be either total or partial (including territory in the area or probable theater of operations), total mobilization of the armed forces is impossible to conceal and may require more time than modern warfare allows (Khorkov 1982: 53–60; Gareyev 1985: 241–43). As a result, peacetime forces can not be just the covering forces for general mobilization as in the past, but must be a portion of the main forces that are deployed and maintained at sufficient force levels and at a high degree of combat readiness (Sokolovskii 1975: 306; Ogarkov 1979: 564). These forces must be able to counter any attack in the initial period of war without the benefit of a prolonged period of total mobilization (Alferov 1981: 33). In addition, based on the experience of the Great Patriotic War, "these forces must also be organized to carry out tasks of both a defensive and offensive nature (Khorkov 1986: 15).

The actual ability and need for mobilization of the forces varies by branch of service. The Strategic Rocket Forces, the Voisk VPK (Air Defense Forces) and the air force are maintained at a combat level and could operate at the outset of the war without major mobilizations. The navy would mobilize by reequipping existing ships, restaffing mothballed vessels and acquiring civilian tonnage, and would require some initial mobilization time to come up to combat strength. The most extensive need for mobilization would be in the ground forces and would be accomplished by the formation of new commands and units by territory (Sokolovskii 1975: 310).

As a result of the problems associated with the beginning period of World War II and the growing probability of an initial conventional phase of any future war, the Soviet General Staff began a renewed study of the beginning period of war in the mid-1960s and early 1970s. The political failure to mobilize in 1941 and the possibility of a protracted war with an initial conventional phase makes the decision to bring the forces to full combat readiness and to employ those forces early on a massive scale a critical factor for the strategic leadership. Ogarkov eloquently described the need for a timely employment of forces in 1979 when he described the dynamic and wide-ranging conditions of the beginning period of a future war by saying that, "Modern operations will be characterized by larger scale and will involve a fierce struggle to seize and retain the strategic initiative, by highly mobile operations of groupings of armed forces on independent axes, under the condition of the absence of continuous fronts . . . and by rapid and abrupt changes in the operational strategic situation" (Ogarkov

1979: 564–67). The concentration on a conventional phase makes mobilization more important and makes it almost certain that the majority of conversions to a war footing will be accomplished during the initial period of hostilities. Therefore the failures of the highly centralized mobilization during World War II should be redressed in contemporary plans and methods.

The system of decentralized mobilization by military districts is more flexible than the system that was in place during the Great Patriotic War. It solves the problem of the transportation of personnel and supplies, creates mobilization stores near troop activation points, and reduces deployment time (Khorkov 1986: 60). The autonomy of territorial commands and their ability to form and field units and create fronts independently is also more sensitive to contemporary warfare, since it disperses men and material over the entire nation and simplifies administration. It makes initial and subsequent wartime mobilizations possible despite the disruption of transportation and communication networks. Territorial mobilization by military districts (sixteen districts, as in the Great Patriotic War) means that the Soviets will have the ability to maintain and use a large, trained reserve force that can be integrated into combat ready units and formations. These reserves are able, therefore, to switch to a war footing in a much shorter period of time.

In order to maintain the autonomy of territorial manning the military districts are solely responsible for planning and implementing military mobilization, registration, premilitary training and the training of inductees and reservists under UMT, call-ups, and the selection of candidates for military schools and special institutes. These tasks are accomplished through the same network of military commissariats in all autonomous republics, krays, oblasts, rayons and cities that existed during the war.

As a result of the wartime experience emphasis has been placed on extensive premilitary training beginning in all secondary schools and continuing through summer sports camps, in vocational and technical institutes, industrial enterprises and universities (Biryuzov 1964: 9). Partially as a result of this extensive preinduction training program, the actual terms of service have been reduced to two to three years, and this, in turn has meant that virtually everyone has some military training. This ensures a vast reserve of military manpower, which is the cornerstone of Soviet mobilization plans.

Beyond assuring that a large reserve exists, the key to military preparedness is a high level of combat readiness. As one Soviet military analyst said, "The degree of combat readiness depends upon the levels of providing the units and formations with personnel, equipment and weapons, upon the supply of material, upon the state of field, air and sea skills and the art and maturity of command personnel" (Lushev 1987: 7). Combat readiness, in contemporary terms, cannot exist without a highly centralized and organized rear (*tyl*) that is organic to units, not merely activated by mobilization, as in the last war; it also cannot exist without highly dispersed and relatively mobile stockpiles of supplies, weapons and fuel. In addition, troops must be highly trained and expediently deployed. The level of combat readiness of the Soviet forces is therefore dependent on preparedness in the long term and the ability to mobilize in the short term. The military potential of the Soviet force is based on the successful combination of these two factors.

Conclusion

It is evident from the study of postwar Soviet writings relating to the mobilization experience that the lessons of planning and implementing the economic and military mobilizations during the war made an indelible impression on contemporary Soviet planners. The possibility of finding themselves in relatively the same position with regard to the need to mobilize rapidly while under fire and amid the potential disruption caused by the use of nuclear weapons, makes the almost pathological study of the Great Patriotic War understandable.

Modern-day military planners have retained the basic methods and structures of the mobilization experience, while adapting them to the requirements and form of war in the modern age. It can be argued, however, that the overall lessons of the war—maintaining economic strength in peacetime, the need for autonomous territorial manning of the forces, and the need for an increased level of combat readiness—would be the logical solutions to the singular problems of mobilizing the nation in response to the "surprise" attack at the start of World War II. In this sense, modernization and technology have had little effect on mobilization.

Planning for the economic and military mobilizations of the present era, therefore, depend on the Soviet's ability to learn from their past, to anticipate and adapt what they can, and to recognize the reality of the costs of preparedness in the face of war.

Notes

The author would like to thank the Center for International Studies at MIT for the support of this project.

1 By the time the German army invaded the Soviet Union in June of 1941 their massed style of blitzkrieg warfare was evident in their campaigns of 1939–40. In addition the premobilization and deployment of the German force left little to the imagination.
2 Khorkov 1987: 15–24; Smirnov 1979: 66–69; Vannikov 1968–69: 116–23; Kurkotin 1984: 3–11.
3 1946–55 was a period of gathering and analyzing data, with doctrine still dependent on Stalin's five permanently operating factors. In 1955 doctrine underwent a period of reevaluation and was changed.
4 As late as May of 1941 the Soviets were still honoring their trade agreements with Germany, shipping them tons of much needed foodstuffs and raw materials.
5 This excerpt is a part of a discussion Brezhnev had regarding the professional military. He stressed the fact that only the political leadership determines policy—even military policy. For a complete look at this see Hyland 1987: 93.
6 For Soviet military responses to crisis based on World War I and World War II models of behavior see Hart 1984: 214–22.
7 Gibson 1983: 141; Zverev 1946: 45, 104. Although planned allocations for 1941 were 71 percent, after the invasion the peak of wartime defense allocations was in 1942–43 with 59 percent. Total defense expenditure included the budget of the army, navy, special troops (NKVD), maintenance of military installations, pay of military personnel, procurement of material and operation of defense plants. Other funds drawn from the other sections of the national economy may also have been used for expanding military readiness before the war.
8 Vannikov 1968–69: 116–23. For a discussion of the expansion of the aviation industry before the war, see Volkov 1979: 57–64.
9 By 1941 these regions contained almost half of the military plants producing 18.5 percent of the defense product.
10 TsGASA (Central State Archives of the Soviet Army) in Khorkov 1987: 15–24. The reserve of machine tools, industrial equipment as well as castings, forgings, inventories of major parts (semifinished products and supply materials) and fuel which were put into the mobilization reserve prior to the war made it possible from the first days of the war to increase armament production at operating plants in extremely short periods of time. In monetary terms the state material reserves over the eighteen months prior to the war rose from four billion rubles to 7.6 billion.

11   Sixty-eight percent of the iron, 58 percent of the steel and 60 percent of the aluminum were cast and 63 percent of the coal was mined in these areas. *Istoriya vtoroi mirovoi voiny 1939–1945* 1975, 4: 152.

12   *Istoriya vtoroi mirovoi voiny 1939–1945* 1982: 4: 144.

13   In 1941 and early 1942, 1,523 industrial enterprises, including 1,360 large military enterprises were evacuated to the east along with ten million workers essential to the country's defense. These figures comprised one third to one half of all key industries and represented more than one million carloads of equipment and materials. Aircraft munitions, machine building, chemical, metallurgical and ordnance plants were evacuated from war zones, reassembled or merged with comparable facilities in the east, and put into operation. New resources and processing plants were developed in these areas since they could not be evacuated.

14   *50 let vooruzhennykh sil'SSSR* 1968: 233.

15   *KPSS: stroitel'stvo vooruzhennky sil SSSR* 1967: 151, 153.

16   In January of 1941 the call-up age was lowered to 19 resulting in a three-year immediate induction.

17   *Sovetskaya voennaya entsiklopediya* 1976: 2: 55; *50 Let.* 1968: 234.

18   *Istoriya velikoi otchestvennoi voiny Sovetskogo Soyuza* 1960: 1: 474.

19   *Istoriya velikoi,* 474.

20   *Sovetskaya voennaya entsiklopediya* 1976: 5: 343.

21   *Sovetskaya voennaya,* 2: 56.

22   *50 let vooruzhennykh sil SSSR* 1968: 273.

23   Sokolovskii 1975: 245. According to the most recent Soviet writings on the beginning period of war, Garayev 1985: 241–43; Alferov 1981: 33, a prolonged period of crisis during which some degree of mobilization of industry and manpower can be accomplished may still be possible in modern warfare. These writings are, however, particularly sensitive to the provocative nature of mobilization during periods of international crisis.

6

The Soviet Defense Industry in War and Peace

Peter Almquist

Since the early 1980s the number of officials moving from the Soviet defense industries into the key positions in the civilian sector has steadily increased, culminating in February 1988 with the promotion of the head of the Military Industrial Commission to chairman of Gosplan and candidate member status on the politburo. Only two months earlier M. S. Gorbachev had held the defense sector up as a model: "Lots of things are done well in the country: Take defense. Here we are not lagging behind in anything. This means that we know how to work" (*Pravda*, 3 October 1987: 2).

Indeed, the defense industrial sector of the Soviet economy apparently does "know how to work," producing hundreds of aircraft and missiles and dozens of ships and submarines each year.[1] It is also frequently claimed that these weapons are of a quality comparable to the best produced in western countries.

How has the Soviet defense industry been able to accomplish so much, especially when it is inextricably linked with an increasingly moribund civilian economy? Much of its success can be attributed to the experiences of the Great Patriotic War in organization, design, and production. Perhaps even more important, many of the key individuals responsible for the Soviet industrial successes of the war continued to hold important posts through the 1980s. The professional lives of these individuals were shaped by their wartime experience, and they continued to have vested interests in applying the lessons of those experiences to the development of the contemporary defense industries in the Soviet Union.

Wartime Defense Organization

One of Stalin's most important legacies was the industrial apparatus he imposed on the Soviet economy: by the late 1930s the Soviet economy was being dragged from a peasant and agrarian economy to a world-class industrial power.

At the same time, the Soviet leadership recognized that war was brewing: whether for ideological reasons (predicting the inevitable assault by capitalist powers), for reasons of *realpolitik*, or as a result of Stalin's personal paranoia, the Soviet Union began to prepare for war. The Second (1933–37) and, in particular, the Third Five-Year Plan (planned for 1938–42) each made significant contributions to the development of the Soviet military base. In the Second Five-Year Plan defense industrial output increased almost twice as fast as civilian production. By 1940 (the middle of the Third Five-Year Plan), almost a third of the state budget (56.8 billion rubles, or 32.6 percent) was allocated to military needs.[2]

Recognition that war was probable led to the formation in April 1937 of a seven-man Soviet Defense Committee, *Komitet oborony SSSR* (KO).[3] The purpose of the KO was to coordinate defense matters and address questions of military-technical support as well as of more general military affairs. "Mobilized stocks, reserves of resources, fuel, provisions, as well as questions of the organization of the fortified areas, lines of defense, naval bases, and the timely preparation of separate branches of industry for production of military goods were considered at meetings of the KO."[4] It was also responsible for overseeing the development of specifications for military equipment and the testing of new equipment.[5]

Within a year, however, the KO apparently determined that it needed an executive agent. On January 31, 1938, the Military Industrial Commission (*Voenno-promyshlennaya komissiya*, or VPK) was established. It was dedicated to the "problems of mobilization and the preparation of all industry to ensure the carrying out of the plans and assignments of the Defense

Committee of the Soviet of People's Commissars on the production of armaments for the Soviet Army and Navy."[6]

Almost nothing else is known about the VPK during this early period, and what it was able to accomplish is unclear, for it appears to have been superseded within two years: from at least 1940 to 1941 there was a Council for Defense Industry attached to the Council of People's Commissars.[7]

With the German attack on the Soviet Union in June 1941, the KO was replaced on June 30 by the State Defense Committee (*Gosudarstvenny komitet oborony*, or GKO), which was charged with the mobilization of all the means and resources and vested with "the full power of the state."[8] Individual members of the GKO apparently had responsibility for various parts of the defense industry: Molotov for tanks, Beria for armaments and munitions, Malenkov for aircraft, and Mikoyan for food and fuel.[9]

On July 4, 1941, the GKO apparently ordered a commission headed by Gosplan chairman N. A. Voznesenskii and including the commissars of the most important industrial ministries to develop a military-economic plan to ensure the supply of hardware to the armed forces.[10] By the end of 1942 the GKO had also established an operational bureau to monitor the ongoing work of each of the defense industrial (and other critical) commissariats.[11]

Regardless of the existence and evolution of a complex of organizations, committees, and commissions, it seems clear that the Soviet defense industry was really operated by the GKO, with Gosplan, the defense industrial commissariats, and other organizations working under it.[12] Voznesenskii was a key member of the GKO from 1942, and through him the GKO reviewed and approved the military production plan on a monthly basis (Kukushkin 1986: 34). The GKO's main role, after all, was to run the support effort for the war; the Supreme High Command (VGK), its STAVKA (headquarters), and the General Staff handled the management of the war itself.

On January 11, 1939 (Shumikhin 1986: 208) the Commissariat of Defense Industry had been split into four separate commissariats: aviation, shipbuilding, ammunition, and armaments.[13] At the beginning of the war, Gosplan also established new economic departments that corresponded with these new commissariats: aviation, shipbuilding, ammunition, tanks, and armaments (Morekhina 1986: 268).

During the war, other commissariats were formed, including the Commissariat of Tank Industry in September 1941, and the Commissariat for Mortars (out of the Commissariat for General Machine Building) two months later.[14] The People's Commissars of these industries were: A. I. Shakhurin for aircraft; I. I. Nosenko for shipbuilding[15]; I. P. Sergeyev, P. N. Goremykin, and B. L. Vannikov for ammunition; D. F. Ustinov for armaments; V. A. Malyshev for tanks, and P. I. Parshin for mortars.

While each of the defense industrial ministries were expanded prior to and in the early stages of the war, it was the aviation industry that was the principal recipient of state largesse. In 1940, 40 percent of the military budget was going towards the development of the Soviet aircraft industry (Shumikhin 1986: 210), and while there were only 14 design bureaus (KBs) with 1,370 workers for the aviation industry in 1936, by 1939 there were 30 KBs with 3,166 employees (Shumikhin 1986: 215). New aircraft factories were built, old ones refurbished, and existing plants converted from other industries.[16]

At the other extreme (and despite the Soviet navy's claims of having played a significant role in the Great Patriotic War), the GKO obviously concluded that the value of producing ships during the war was minimal, and directed scarce materials to more critical (and time-urgent) weapons systems. From July to December 1941, 35 military ships were produced, and the number rapidly declined to 15 in 1942, 14 in 1943, 4 in 1944, and only 2 in 1945.[17]

The Communist party (then still referred to as the All-Union Communist Party [Bolshevik], or VKP[b]) was also a significant organizational actor in the defense industries. Like so many state bodies, it reorganized during the war, even though the Party and government were probably more closely interlocked than ever before or after. For example, *oblast* and republic first secretaries were designated GKO representatives in their regions (Ivashov 1987: 38).

Special departments of the Central Committee were apparently established to oversee parts of the defense industry. Again, the aircraft industry was a focus of attention: in 1942 the Central Committee established departments for aircraft building (headed by A. V. Budnikov) and for engine building (headed by G. M. Grigor'yan), which were apparently merged in 1942 into a Department of Aviation Industry under Grigor'yan.[18] In several *gorkoms* (city committees) and *obkoms* (regional committees), the post of Secretary for Aviation Industry was established in early 1940 (Shumikhin 1986: 208). It is not clear whether there were other departments for other branches, although the industrial departments of the various party organizations were often reorganized to better oversee defense production.[19]

In addition, the VKP(b) could rely on its network of party organizers at various plants. The position of "partorg" had been instituted in 1932 to enforce Party leadership and to guide work at important facilities. With the beginning of the war, there were partorgs at 1,170 of the most important enterprises, research institutes, and other facilities.[20]

During the prewar period the military had also been preparing for war, striving to make procurement more efficient. M. N. Tukhachevskii, perhaps the most important prewar Soviet military thinker (he was executed in 1937 during the Great Purges), had been appointed deputy commissar for armaments in 1931, with the task of developing a modern (and, in particular, mobile) military. During his tenure, Tukhachevskii oversaw the establishment of a number of the most important design bureaus or saw to the training of several future designers: gun designers such as Degtyarev, Tokarev, Shpital'ny; artillery designers Makhanov, Magdoseyev, Sidorenko, Gavrilov, Grabin, Ivanov, Petrov; tank designers Barykov, Ginsburg, Kozyrev, Lebedev, Toskin, Firsov; aircraft designers Tupolev, Polikarpov, Grigorovich, and Mikulin; and the original rocket design bureaus (Ivanov 1985: 280–86).

During the war the role of Deputy Commissar for Armaments was probably taken by G. I. Kulik, who was also head of the Main Artillery Administration (*Glavnoye artilleriyckoye upravleniye*, or GAU) starting in 1939. GAU was responsible for the development of technical requirements, the testing of new artillery, and its introduction into the arsenal.[21] While the armed services were responsible for providing design requirements, it seems clear that the prevailing attitude was to do little that would jeopardize current production in order to improve a weapon. In order to maintain production levels, the transition time from one weapon system to another at a plant had to be kept at the absolute minimum.

Monitoring the production for the military administrations were the military representatives (*voenny predstavitel'*, or *voyenpred*), an institution since Peter the Great. The *voyenpred* is an officer or employee of the armed forces assigned to a defense plant to ensure against deviations from assigned requirements and to act as a monitor of the quality level at the plant (Mikoyan, for example, was a *voyenpred* prior to his appointment as deputy chief of an aircraft design bureau). The *voyenpred* network was clearly extensive; in 1942 the GAU had 1,300 military personnel and 13,000 civilians (*vol'nonayommy*) working as *voyenpred*, monitoring the production of hundreds of thousands of guns, mortars, and artillery pieces.[22]

The prewar and wartime structure established by the Soviets accomplished what it was designed to do. First, it mobilized and concentrated resources into those industries deemed critical for the Soviet defense effort. These industries, in turn, were able to produce weapons in large numbers, meeting military requirements, and on fairly short notice (see Table 6.1). The success of the Soviets

Table 6.1
Production of Military Equipment

	June–December 1941	1942	1943	1944	January–August 1945	Total
Rifles and carbines (1000s)	1,567	4,049	3,436	2,450	637	12,139
Submachine-guns (1000s)	89	1,506	2,023	1,970	583	6,173
Machine-guns (1000s)	106	356	458	439	156	1,515
Ordnance (1000s)	30	127	130	122	72	482
Mortars (1000s)	42	230	69	7	3	351
Tanks and SP artillery (1000s)	4	24	24	29	20	102
Combat aircraft (1000s)	8	21	29	33	19	112
Combat ships	35	15	14	4	2	70

Source: Vtoraya Mirovaya Voina: itoqi i uroki (Moscow: Voyenizdat, 1985), 229.

in stopping the Nazi drive and launching a counteroffensive further sanctified the Soviet structure. The fact that many of those in key positions at the time were relatively young and would lead the Soviet Union over the next forty years only reinforced the trend.

After the war and into the early 1960s several changes in Soviet defense industry took place. At the most senior level, a defense council, headed by the General Secretary and apparently including senior government and Party officials, was established, presumably in the 1950s. A Communist Party of the Soviet Union (CPSU) secretary with responsibility for defense industry (or "new technology") was also appointed. The first secretary to have this post was probably L. I. Brezhnev who held the post from 1956 to 1960, and again from 1963 until his appointment as First Secretary (the title was changed to General Secretary in 1966) in 1964. He was replaced as secretary for defense industry by Ustinov, who had been Minister of Armaments until 1957 and then probably the chairman of the VPK.

Gosplan apparently received a permanent first deputy chairman responsible for defense industry in the early 1960s.[23] Since 1962 the deputies have been V. M. Ryabikov (1962–74), G. A. Titov (1974–80), L. A. Voronin (1980–82), Yu. D. Maslyukov (1982–85), and V. I. Smyslov, a former Deputy Minister of shipbuilding.[24] Within Gosplan there is reportedly a summary department for national economic planning for defense industry,[25] which oversees about ten branch departments responsible for the defense industrial ministries.

Immediately after the war the Soviet defense industries were consolidated into three ministries: shipbuilding, aviation industry, and armaments. Ustinov continued as Minister of Armaments, while other defense industry officials were moved into other important positions. For example, V. A. Malyshev took over the newly formed State Committee on Technology (*Gostekhnika*). *Gostekhnika* oversaw the development of a range of new technologies, including space flight, rocketry, and nuclear power.[26] B. L. Vannikov, Commissar of Ammunition during the war, played a leading role in the nuclear weapons program until he retired in 1958.

New ministries were established to provide the expanded industrial base necessary for new military technologies. The Ministry of Medium Machine Building was established in 1953 to oversee the development of nuclear weapons. The Ministry of General Machine Building was established in 1965 for production of missiles. And in 1968 the Ministry of Machine Building was established from out of the Ministry of Defense Industry, with responsibility for conventional weapons, munitions, and solid propellants. In addition, other ministries were established with responsibility for electronics and communications work (much of it defense related): the Ministry of Radio Industry (established in 1954), the Ministry of Electronics Industry (established in 1961), and the Ministry of Communications Equipment Industry (established in 1974).

In 1947 the Ministry of Defense reestablished the post of Deputy Minister for Armaments. It was held by Artillery Marshal N. D. Yakovlev (1947–52), then Artillery Marshal M. I. Nedelin (1952–53, 1955–59). Both officers were closely involved with the development of missiles, and Nedelin was appointed in 1959 as the first commander in chief of the Strategic Rocket Forces.[27] From 1953 there also was a Deputy Minister of Defense for radar and radioelectronics: A. I. Berg from 1953 to 1957 and A. V. Gerasimov from 1957 to 1964. In 1964 Gerasimov became First Deputy Chief of the General Staff for Armaments. The post of Deputy Minister for Armaments does not reappear until 1970, when N. N. Alekseyev was called back from the SALT talks, which had just started, to take the post (Smith 1985: 48). V. V. Druzhinin, a specialist in radar and air defense, replaced Alekseyev as deputy chief of the General Staff and head of its Scientific-Technical Committee.[28] The changing backgrounds of the post's occupants neatly frame the evolving priorities of the Soviet armed forces, moving from missiles (when this was a high-priority item) to specialists in electronics (as this became increasingly important).

In the CPSU apparatus a Department of Defense Industry was apparently added in early 1958, it was presumably broken off from the Heavy Industry Department and headed by I. D. Serbin.[29] In addition, similar departments were established in republics and *oblasts*.[30]

Lessons for the Development of the Contemporary Soviet Defense Industry

In the Soviet view, the Great Patriotic War confirmed the superiority of the Soviet socialist system for developing a defense base for war.[31] First, the concentration of production in a relatively small number of large enterprises (many situated close to resources) ensured the benefits of operating on large scale. Second, the planning system allowed for the rapid redirection of resources and materiel. Finally, the Soviets were able to use those resources more efficiently than the enemy.[32] But in addition to these general "lessons," the Soviets drew some specific conclusions about weapons design and production from their wartime experience.

In the 1960s the Soviets began to pay increasing attention to the benefits of systems analysis in weapons procurement. With Khrushchev's wholesale cutting and redirecting of resources and the increasingly expensive high technology weapons (such as missiles), it is not surprising that the Soviets began to seek a more scientific approach to the issue of resource allocation. As one Soviet author noted, "Here we have the problem of value optimum calculations, economic modelling and qualitative analysis . . ." (Korniyenko 1967: 62–65).

Such analysis has to account for three critical factors in weapons acquisition: timeliness, cost, and effectiveness (Sarkisian and Starik 1985: 260–68). Political and economic circumstances determine which of these factors takes precedence at any given time. During the Great Patriotic War time was clearly the most important factor. A weapon had to be effective, of course, and its production costs had to be kept as low as possible, but with the Nazis already occupying Soviet territory, rapidly getting the weapon off the drawing board and into the hands of the Soviet soldier was the overriding objective.

This need for timeliness reinforced an existing tendency towards incremental development in Soviet weapons design and production. As one Soviet author argued, "when designing original and improving existing means of combat, it is very important to achieve their qualitative change [through] *design transformations*" (emphasis added, Kalerin 1965:17). A major technological breakthrough was to take second place to incremental development, which produced a more reliable system and was a safer investment. As a result, three main themes appear regularly in Soviet discussions of weapons design: producibility, standardization, and unification.[33]

The memoirs of weapons designers of the Great Patriotic War and the postwar period emphasize the importance of being able to design and produce weapons systems rapidly.[34] Many of these memoirs appeared at a time when the Soviets were developing production associations (*Proizvodstvennoye ob'edineniye*, POs, or *vsesoyuznoye proizvodstvennoye ob'edineniye*, VPOs) and scientific production associations in an effort to integrate science and production more effectively. The memoirs of these designers are consistent with the views that one might expect to find in support of these associations. In particular, the emphasis on close links between designers and engineers fits with the common theme in the recollections of the military designers.

As is so often the case, the Soviets have pursued administrative solutions to productivity problems: design bureaus and production facilities are collocated, a process that was common during the war, and designers are expected to pay close attention to the actual production of their product. Designers are generally sent to the plants as series production is beginning, and they continually monitor production as it continues.[35]

The work of V. G. Grabin, head of the Central Artillery Design Bureau during the war, is frequently held up as a model of production efficiency.[36] Grabin developed a fast production technique that relied on the close cooperation between the designer and the engineer. "In trying to reduce the time for manufacture, the design bureau of V. G. Grabin began to make wide use of the consultations of technologists in the course of planning. This, it would appear, simple solution immediately led to stunning results . . ." (Karnozov 1970: 43–44). In his own recollections of the experiences of the Great Patriotic War Grabin drew attention to how the close ties between designer and engineer that were established during the war had substantially degenerated by 1969 (Kudrevatykh 1969: 168–74).

One of the keys to ensuring productivity, particularly in the defense industries, is the process of unification and standardization (*unifikatsiya i standartizatsiya*).[37] While producibility may be one of the most important factors, if not the most important factor, in designing new weapons systems, unification and standardization form its basis. As a biographer of aircraft designer P. O. Sukhoi noted, "At the end of the 1960s in our country serious attention turned to the long-range development in industry of standardization and unification as effective means of accelerating scientific-technical progress" (Kuz'mina 1985: 219–20).

Codified into law in the early 1970s, unification tries to reduce the number of parts to a minimum set that can be used in a wide range of weapons systems. The number of specialized parts required for a particular weapon system is thus minimized. Standardization is the establishment of norms and indicators based on contemporary production and design capabilities to ensure that parts are uniform and to encourage the application of existing technology in new ways.[38] There are four levels of standards: State

(GOST), Branch (OST), Republic (RST) and local (that is, at the plant or organization—STP).

A component can be designed to be so flexible that it can be used in a number of different pieces of equipment, but this may increase its cost substantially or, in some circumstances, reduce its effectiveness. On the other hand, a component can be designed so it is useful in only one weapon system. The goal of unification is to avoid these extremes and thus help balance the cost of the weapon system and the weapon's required effectiveness.[39]

The greatest application of unification has been in the machine building and instrument making industries, the two leading sectors of the economy for defense production.[40] In addition to applying to pieces of production equipment, unification also refers to the use of the same military technology in different weapon systems or in different branches of the armed forces.[41] A good example is probably the use of SS-16 ICBM components for SS-20 IRBM,[42] but there are also examples in which a weapon developed for use by one service has been adapted by another. For example, the Soviet SA-8 antiaircraft system, used by the ground forces, uses the same missile as that used in the navy's SA-N-4 antiaircraft system (see Taylor 1986: 83–98).

Design unification tries to minimize the numbers of types and designs of products, components, and basic materials used in designing a weapons system. Design unification is considered especially relevant to the development of new technology and work in scientific research and experimental-design work. Production unification is intended to minimize the varieties of raw material or subcomponents necessary to produce a finished article.[43]

Standardization and unification are especially common in writings about the artillery industry. The two leading artillery designers of the Great Patriotic War, F. F. Petrov and V. G. Grabin, emphasized the importance of unification and standardization to production, as do a number of unsigned editorials in the military press.[44] As Petrov noted in 1965, "I wish to stress once more the important role played by the unification and standardization of all military equipment and armament. This cannot be overestimated, especially in connection with series production."[45] Grabin, recalling a case from the Great Patriotic War, emphasized that "the unification of the parts, units, mechanisms, and assemblies [in the new USV cannon] permitted not only a significant reduction of the time for planning, making, developing, and testing the experimental model, but an acceleration of the process of setting up serial production."[46]

Similarly, Zhosef Kotin, perhaps the leading tank designer of the Great Patriotic War, emphasized in the mid-1970s the reliance his designers placed on "the wise use of the principle of unification [which] made an enormous contribution to the development of the tank industry in wartime."[47] And the developments of G. S. Shpagin, a heavy machine gun designer, and S. G. Simonov, another machine gun designer, were also praised because of the emphasis they placed on the producibility of these weapons.[48] One of the points made in a discussion of the development of small arms in general is the need to have "extreme simplification in production technology, which aids in processing parts with machine tools used in the production of non-military products" (Kosyrev 1971: 8–11).

It would be easy to dismiss Soviet interest in standardization and unification as just rhetoric and common sense, but it is striking how much emphasis is placed on this issue. As *Tekhnika i vooruzheniye* emphasized in discussing artillery development during the war,

> the task was set to implement one of the most important principles for design engineering—standardization of the designs of those parts, assemblies, and mechanisms which had recommended themselves well in artillery weapons and ammunition, that is, which had already been proven on proving grounds and in the troops.[49]

The emphasis on unification and standardization was not simply in the relatively low technology fields such as artillery, but also in aviation and missiles. Sukhoi had a special unification brigade established in his design bureau (Kuz'mina 1985: 219–20). In his designs, like so many designers, he was already practicing the unification and standardization that was being institutionalized. One Western analyst characterizes Sukhoi's designs as "classic examples" of the use of concurrent and previous designs on current prototypes, citing the common wing, tails, and cockpit of two different Sukhoi fighters as but one example.[50]

In the missile field, Yangel (who died in 1971) is held up as a model in his judicious experimentation with the use of unification in developing rockets and missiles through the 1960s (Platonov and Gorbulin 1979: 78–81). An unusual example (for the Soviet literature) of unification is included in V. P. Mishin's discussion of rocket and missile design, where he provides a chart showing the derivation of a number of boosters from the first Soviet ICBM, the SS-6 (Mishin 1985: 17). And the case of the SS-13 and SS-16 and their derivatives, both designed by A. D. Nadiradze, has already been noted.

It should also be recalled that most defense industrial plants are dual purpose, producing for both military and civilian customers.[51] As one military author has noted, the civilian component of a defense plant is principally designed to make productive peacetime use of space that would be necessary in the event of mobilization.[52]

During peacetime pursuing standardization and unification makes good economic sense, just as doing so made sense for reasons of timeliness in the Great Patriotic War. When the Soviets apparently undertook a major effort to contain costs in the early 1970s, they were able to turn directly to the lessons of the Great Patriotic War for their cost-saving implications. Beginning in 1974, according to Western intelligence estimates, the growth of Soviet military procurement "dropped markedly," apparently as a result of a policy decision.[53] Several factors, including the length of time of the slowdown and the absence of new resources allocated to overcome any bottlenecks that might have been responsible, indicate that the decline was a result of a conscious decision, rather than simply the result of procurement cycles or a temporary problem. One other set of indicators should be mentioned: the officials responsible for defense production suffered no repercussions under four different general secretaries. In fact, many were moved into problem areas of the civilian economy in an apparent effort to improve those trouble areas.

At the time of any probable decision to slow defense procurement, the Secretary for Defense Industry was D. F. Ustinov, Minister of Armaments in the Great Patriotic War. The Gosplan official responsible for defense industry was G. A. Titov, deputy commissar for shipbuilding during the war. General Secretary Brezhnev had been the first postwar secretary for defense industry. It is not surprising that these men fell back on experiences from thirty years earlier in viewing how to make the defense economy more efficient. Opposition to the cuts, certain to be expressed by the military, may help explain the appointment of Ustinov, first to the politburo in March 1976, and then, one month later, to the post of Minister of Defense upon Grechko's unexpected death.[54]

Conclusion

As a result of their experiences in the Great Patriotic War, the Soviets developed a system of defense production and procurement that was capable of providing a continuing flow of weapons (in peacetime) to the armed forces. The system was put in place and maintained by a number of people who had firsthand experience with the mechanisms used in the war, and who survived to manage the war economy into the 1970s and 1980s.

While the driving force behind the defense industries in the Great Patriotic War was the need for large numbers of weapons in the shortest time possible, the 1970s and 1980s shifted the battlefield to an economic one. The cost of increasingly complex weapons systems was becoming the major enemy, and this was a struggle that the Soviets were in real danger of losing. Their economy was barely able to sustain itself, let alone undertake the investment needed to supply the weapons that were foreseen as potentially decisive in a future war. The defense industries were called upon to save resources and to be ever more efficient.

In the struggle for savings and efficiency the defense industries have adapted the lessons learned during the war. The successes of the defense industries have made them the model against which the civilian sector is compared. The new State Acceptance Service is clearly based on the *voyenpred* system, and the new leaders of the civilian economy are increasingly being plucked from the defense industries.

The Great Patriotic War and the experience of the last forty years seem to prove that the defense industries did, as Gorbachev suggests, "know how to work." Whether Gorbachev can apply the lessons of the defense industries to the Soviet economy as a whole, however, remains to be seen.

Notes

1   For production estimates, see U.S. Department of Defense (annual volumes); U.S. Congress 1984a; and U.S. Congress 1984b: 17.

2   Kukushkin 1986: 22–23; *Velikaya Otechestvennaya Voina Sovetskogo Soyuza, 1941–1945: Kratkaya Istoriya* 1984: 40.

3   The Soviets have had some type of senior defense organization since 1918, when the Council of Worker and Peasant Defense (or Defense Council) was formed. It was reorganized in 1920 as the Council of Labor and Defense. This council, in turn, was replaced in April 1937 by the Defense Committee. The period after the war is less clear, although it is known that the current organ (the Defense Council) has existed since at least 1957. See Golubovich 1984: 207.

4   *Sovetskaya voennaya entsiklopediya*, vol. 4 1977: 266.

5   The KO comprised Stalin, Voroshilov (from 1940), Malenkov, Mikoyan, Molotov, Voznesenskii, Zhdanov, and Beria. See Jerry F. Hough, "The Historical Legacy in Soviet Weapons Development," in Valenta and Potter 1984: 90.

6   *Sovetskaya voennaya entsiklopediya*, vol. 4 1977: 266. See also the decree establishing the VPK, reprinted in *KPSS o vooruzhennykh silakh Sovetskogo Soyuza: dokumenty, 1917–1981* 1981: 268.

7   The entry on P. N. Goremykin in the *Encyclopedia of the Great Patriotic War* refers to his work on the *Sovet po oboronnoy promyshlennosti pri SNK*. See *Velikaya Otechestvennaya Voina Sovetskogo Soyuza, 1941–1945: Entsiklopediya* 1985: 213.

8   *Voennye voprosy v dokumentakh KPSS i Sovetskogo gosudarstva* 1980: 30. The GKO originally included politburo members and candidate members Stalin, Molotov, Voroshilov, Malenkov, and Beria. It was later expanded to include Kaganovich, Mikoyan, Bulganin, and Voznesenskii. Vernon V. Aspaturian, "The Stalinist Legacy in Soviet National Decisionmaking," in Valenta and Potter 1984: 54.

9   Schapiro 1971: 499. Hough notes that members of the Politburo also seemed to have responsibilities in several sectors, with Zhdanov overseeing tanks, Malenkov (in at least one case) for mortars, and Stalin for aircraft. See Hough in Valenta and Potter 1984: 90.

10 Hough refers to this as the Economic Council for Defense Industry, although the original reference does not capitalize it, and identifies it as *khozyaystvenny sovet oboronnoy promyshlennosti*. See Chalmayev 1978: 100.

11 V. A. Yezhov, "Upravleniye narodnym khozyaystvom v gody Velikoy Otechestvennoy Voyny," in Fedoseyev 1987: 312.

12 I. M. Golushko, "Tyl Sovetskih vooruzhennykh sil kak svyazuyushcheye zveno fronta c ekonomicheskoy strany v gody voyny," in Fedoseyev 1987: 260.

13 *Voennye voprosy v dokumentakh KPSS i Sovetskogo gosudarstva* 1980: 331. It is not clear if a Commissariat of Defense Industry continued to exist. B. L. Vannikov's biography in *Sovetskaya voennaya entsiklopediya* states that he headed this commissariat from 1939 to 1941.

14 *Velikaya Otechestvennaya Voina Sovetskogo Soyuza, 1941–1945: Entsiklopediya* 1985: 446, 705.

15 Nosenko was simultaneously First Deputy Commissar for the Tank Industry in 1941 and 1942. See *Velikaya Otechestvennaya Voina Sovetskogo Soyuza, 1941–1945: Entsiklopediya* 1985: 497.

16 See *Vtoraya mirovaya voina: itogi i uroki* 1985: 219; A. G. Khorkov 1987: 18–19; Bartenev 1986: 286.

17   *Vtoraya mirovaya voina: itogi i uroki* 1985: 229.
18   Shakhurin 1983: 148–49. Aviation industry departments were also established
      at the republic and *oblast* levels.
19   For example, the Chelyabinsk Obkom had 24 departments, including ones for
      defense, tank, ammunition, and aircraft. See Morekhina 1986: 79.
20   See *Velikaya Otechestvennaya Voina 1941–1945: Entsiklopediya* 1985: 550;
      and Ivashov 1987: 38. Several of the *partorgs* achieved senior positions in later
      years. For example, V. M. Ryabikov (*partorg* at the "Bolshevik" artillery plant
      in Leningrad while Ustinov was its director) went on to become First Deputy
      Chairman of Gosplan, responsible for defense industry, L. N. Yefremov
      (*partorg* at an aircraft plant) went on to become a deputy chief of the State
      Committee on Science and Technology and S. A. Skachkov (who had been at
      a tank plant) was appointed chairman of the State Committee on Foreign
      Economic Relations in 1958.
21   For a good discussion of the administrations, see Hough in Valenta and Potter
      1984: 96–100.
22   I. I. Volkotrubenko, *Voenno-istoricheskii zhurnal* 1986: 94.
23   It may have been earlier, with the appointment of M. V. Khrunichev to the post
      in 1957. Defense industrial officials had been playing a role in various economic
      oversight organizations throughout the myriad of reorganizations and reforms
      of the 1950s. For a good discussion, see John McDonnell, "The Soviet Defense
      Industry as a Pressure Group," in MacGwire et al. 1975: 87–122. Interestingly,
      the first deputy chairman responsible for Defense Industry during the
      Brezhnev era was usually the only Gosplan deputy also to have a seat on the
      Central Committee.
24   Ryabikov had been the *partorg* at the Bolshevik plant in Leningrad, where
      Ustinov was director immediately before the war. Titov was a deputy minister
      of shipbuilding. Voronin, Maslyukov, and Smyslov are too young.
25   The chief of this department from 1977 to his death in 1985 was N. P.
      Marakhovskii, who, according to his obituary, had been a Gosplan defense
      industry specialist for 31 years. See *Izvestiya* 18 October 1985, 6.
26   Chalmayev 1978: 312. Chalmayev characterizes *Gostekhnika* as a "Gosplan for
      new technology" and a "general staff of scientific-technical thought."
27   David Holloway, "Innovation in the Defence Sector," in Amann and Cooper
      1982: 322, 328.
28   The current (since Alekseyev's death in 1980) Deputy Minister for Armaments,
      V. M. Shabanov, also apparently worked in air defense electronics.
29   Serbin had been in Party work since the war. At his death in 1981 he was replaced
      by I. F. Dmitriyev, a wartime deputy of Ustinov's.
30   For example, the Ukraine's Department of Defense Industry was headed from
      its establishment in February 1959 to the mid-1970s by Yakov Kuz'mich
      Rudenko. See *XXIII s'ezd kommunisticheskoi partii Ukrainy: materialy
      s'yezda* 1967: 177; Firdman 1985: 63.
31   For more detail about contemporary Soviet defense industry, see Almquist
      1987.
32   For these "lessons," see *Vtoraya mirovaya voina: itogi i uroki* 1985: 231.
33   The emphasis on the three main themes appears to be greater in the military
      production sphere than in the civilian, possibly because there is a strong

customer (the Ministry of Defense) pushing for actual production of the weapon system.

34 This theme also appears in writings on contemporary weapons development. For example, see Kauk 1976: 45.

35 See, for example, L. Yevtukhov, "Dykhaniye goryachey broni," *Krasnaya zvezda* February 1977.

36 See Grabin 1969:16–17; Karnozov 1970:43–44; Grabin 1970:7; and Tsygankov 1978: 6–13.

37 Both words can be translated as "standardization," but to emphasize the difference between the two, "unification" and "standardization" will be used.

38 Vlasov and Kats 1985: 96–97. See also *Sovetskaya voennaya entsiklopidiya*, vol. 7 1979: 525. The latter article is attributed to N. N. Alekseyev, then Deputy Minister of Defense for Armaments.

39 *Sovetskaya voennaya entsiklopediya*, vol. 8 1980: 199–200.

40 "Unifikatsiya," in *Bol'shaya Sovetskaya Entsiklopediya*, vol. 27, 1977: 23–24.

41 *Sovetskaya voennaya entsiklopediya*, 1980: 199–200.

42 The SS-20 is based on two stages of the SS-X-16. The same technique of using two of the three stages of an ICBM had been used in the late 1960s to create two unsuccessful IRBMs—the SS-X-14 and SS-X-15—from the SS-13 ICBM.

43 Design unification was the only topic discussed in the open press by chief of the Ministry of Defense's Main Technical Administration Yu. D. Maslyukov. Maslyukov went on to become chairman of the VPK from 1985 to 1988, and is currently chairman of Gosplan. See Maslyukov 1978: 15–16. For other discussions, see Vlasov and Kats 1985: 96; Nikiforenko 1975: 4–6; Saksonov 1971: 122–25; Saksonov 1972: 27; and Mishin 1985: 295–96.

44 See, in particular, Petrov 1965: 12–19; Grabin 1970: 7; and Tsygankov 1978: 6–13.

45 Petrov 1965: 18. Petrov repeatedly emphasized the use of the same or similar equipment in different situations, for example, the same basic gun barrel being used in a number of different pieces of artillery.

46 Grabin 1969: 16. In the USV cannon, more than 50 percent of the parts, units, and mechanisms from the existing F-22 were utilized.

47 Saltykov 1975: 7. At the time, Kotin was a member of the Ministry of Defense Industry's Scientific-Technical Council and had spent four years (1967–71) as deputy minister.

48 Sergeyev 1970: 27; and "Oruzhiye dostoynoye boytsa" (1977): 27.

49 "Period perevooruzheniya" 1974: 18–19. The article is a discussion of the contribution of V. D. Grendal', commander of the Main Artillery Administration immediately before the Great Patriotic War. For another example, see "Proizvodstvo artillerskiyskogo vooruzheniya, 1941–1945," 1974: 12–13.

50 Ward 1981:32. Ward also cites a number of other examples from various design bureaus. See also Biery 1983; and Alexander 1981.

51 Julian Cooper, "The Civilian Production of the Soviet Defence Industry," in Amann and Cooper 1986: 31–50.

52 V. Gavrilov noted that this was indicated in the Central Committee report at the Twenty-fourth Party Congress, presumably referring to Brezhnev's statement that 42 percent of the defense industry output is for civilian use. See Gavrilov 1972: 14.

53   Given that the slowdown appeared in about 1974, it most likely was planned
     somewhat earlier. Richard Kaufman suggests that it was the result of decisions
     included in the Ninth Five-Year Plan (1971–76). Regardless of when it was
     planned, Ustinov would have been a key actor in the decisions. See Kaufman
     1985: 221. Ustinov's biography notes his contribution to the economic
     potential of the nation. See *Sovetskaya voennaya entsiklopediya*, vol. 8 1980:
     227. Also see the CIA and DIA report in U.S. Congress 1984b: 5, in which the
     agencies note that the drop in procurement "held overall defense growth
     (measured in dollars) to about 2 percent per year during the 1974–1985 period—
     about half the rate of the previous decade."

54   It is difficult to characterize the views of Ustinov. For two recent attempts to
     do so, see Strode and Strode 1983, and Wettig and Weickhardt 1985. One of
     the few points upon which Wettig and Weickhardt agree is the hard-line stance
     taken by Grechko. While Ustinov may not have been the strongest advocate
     of Soviet arms control, he may have been a reluctant advocate who recognized
     the problems that were beginning to appear in the Soviet economy.

7

Soviet Wartime Decision Making and Control

Daniel McIntosh

The existence of the Soviet state is directly linked to success and failure in war. It was born in the failure of the First World War, originally structured in the crisis of the Civil War, reorganized in anticipation of the Second World War, and further shaped into the superpower we see today by the experience of the Great Patriotic War. The wartime experience has created and continues to legitimize a structure of decision making and control that remains at the core of the Soviet system.

The structure of the government and the party and the planned transformation of that structure in wartime demonstrates a recognition by the Soviet strategic leadership (*strategicheskoye rukovodstvo*) that future wars, whether conventional or nuclear, will be shaped by both technical and political constraints. The system of command in war will reflect the dialectical relationship between ends and means and will require robust mechanisms for operational and political control.

The Second World War provides an unparalleled example of Soviet decision making in time of war. Moreover, the experience of the Great Patriotic War continues to color Soviet perceptions of the tasks that they expect to face in the future. To be sure, a future war will not be a replay of the Second World War. Soviet strategy and the organization of the Soviet state continue to evolve to meet these new challenges. The political and military structures created to meet the requirements of the Stalinist state in World War II, however, continue to serve as the foundation for current Soviet mechanisms of decision making and control.

A Focus on the Soviet State

There is an understandable tendency to focus on the present and the future in order to anticipate—and, if possible, counter—the next Soviet action. To focus on the problems of the 1980s and 1990s without an awareness of their historical context, however, would be to deny one of the most important factors involved in the understanding of Soviet military affairs.

A key to such an analysis is to focus on the evolving structure and processes of the Soviet state.[1] The Soviet state—by which I mean the integrated body of Party and government—is neither a passive arena for pluralist conflict resolution or an infinitely flexible tool for totalitarian control. Instead, the state serves as an objective policy culture that shapes meanings and distributes power, making some actions likely and others all but impossible.[2]

Three elements of this approach are of particular importance. The first is a sensitivity to the unanticipated consequences of action. The creation of structure reflects values and principles. Once it is in place, however, objective structure takes on a life of its own. It supports—or fails to support—values, decisions, and policies that were never considered when the structure was created.

The second element involves the codetermination of agency and structure. Structures create agents: they recruit, test, organize, and socialize the human actors that support the continued existence of a particular set of roles and institutions. Agents can play their roles in a number of ways, however. The choices made by key individuals can in some circumstances transform the structure in which they operate.

Third is the emphasis on the catalytic role of historical crises. In order to endure, a state must identify and surmount both internal and external threats. In the most extreme circumstances nothing short of a radical transformation of state structure may suffice. If such a transformation is achieved, the revised structure—and an associated set of principles and processes expressed in that structure —become the new norm.

Short of an obvious failure to deal with a new crisis, there is little motivation and less leeway for significant structural change. At most, new problems promote minor reforms. More likely, as a state continues to devote its resources to routinized tasks, it runs the risk that new problems may not even be perceived.

For the Soviet Union, there has been no crisis to compare with the Great Patriotic War. Between 1941 and 1945 roughly twenty million soldiers and civilians died. One in three Soviet citizens was killed or wounded, and 80 percent of the man-made structures of the USSR was damaged or destroyed (Baxter 1986: 56–57). Prior to the war, the purges had already decimated the senior officer corps, and with it much of the corporate memory of the Soviet armed forces.[3] Thus, the war demanded expertise and clear lines of authority at a time when both were only beginning to be restored. Having to cope with such a disaster, let alone to triumph, leaves its mark not only on a generation, but on the structure of the state itself.

Contemporary Challenges

At present, the strategic leadership finds itself facing a set of difficult problems. Yet the form of these problems is not entirely new. In order to make sense of complexity, the strategic leadership has turned to the lessons of the past and has found that in many ways the closest Soviet analogue to the 1990s are the years prior to the Great Patriotic War.

As in the period before World War II, the essence of the problem is defined as the impact of new technologies on the conduct and control of military action. Marshal Ogarkov, for example, following his oft-cited description of the current "revolutionary . . . upheaval in military affairs," has immediately and explicitly noted the parallels between the contemporary situation and the 1930s (Ogarkov 1982: 31–32).

During the 1930s the threat from Germany prompted two lines of action. The first was a doubling of the share of the GNP expended on the military in peacetime, a trend that has generally continued to this day (Kohler 1980: 137). Second, and equally important, were the formal organizational changes, including the restoration of the traditional structure of ranks and the establishment of the General Staff. Today economic constraints make it difficult to imagine a comparable increase in available resources. The concern with organizational development, however, continues to be a common theme in Soviet military literature.

This concern is linked to a perception by Soviet military scientists that over the past fifty years the need to gain and keep the initiative has grown ever stronger. A recent Soviet review of the importance of the initial period of war, for example, begins with and draws heavily upon the experience of the world wars. Current technical and operational trends are perceived to "all the more increase the role of the factor of surprise" now and in the future. The ultimate example of the importance of the initial period of war, however, is the disaster of 1941 (Yevseyev 1985: 20).

Today decisions must be made quickly, and missions "will be carried out in a matter of minutes." Thus, there is a "necessity to have in times of peace organs of control capable of functioning immediately at the start of the war, without a long period of reorganization."[4]

The Soviet state has long accepted as a key lesson of history that it functions in a hostile environment. The Great Patriotic War serves to confirm that lesson for the present. There continue to be powerful adversaries to hold in check, and the possibility of a bolt-out-of-the-blue, although not considered a likely scenario for war initiation, remains one of the most stressing. More plausible in Soviet eyes is the possibility of political surprise—as when Stalin discounted indications of the impending German invasion.

To ensure its survival the Soviet state has institutionalized sensitivity to several kinds of threats—not merely the obvious military manifestations, but also the political, social, and economic components of the overall correlation of forces—and remains prepared to respond at short notice. This definition of the situation is in large part a product of, and legitimized by, the wartime experience. This state structure attempts to deal with the threat even as it encourages the threat to be perceived.

The Structural Context

The system of decision making and control at the center of the Soviet state has developed since the wartime experience. In its

essence, however, it remains the objective organizational manifestation of the lessons of World War II.

The upper echelons of this structure are known as the strategic
leadership. In terms of function, a standard Soviet definition of the
strategic leadership describes it as "the activity of the higher
political and military organs for control of the armed forces."[5] In
organizational terms, the strategic leadership operates through the
High Command, General Staff, and "other organs," including
"central command points" and "means of communications,
control (*upravleniye*) and security" (Danilov 1987: 26).

At the summit only one body serves as both a subcommittee of
the Politburo and as a government organ in its own right: the
Defense Council of the USSR. The Defense Council was given
constitutional status as a state organ in the Soviet Constitution of
1977, but it has actually existed since at least 1957.[6] Soviet sources
give little information on its membership. It is known that the
General Secretary of the CPSU automatically assumes the role of
chairman of the Defense Council, and has done so since at least
1964.[7] The other members of the council are a subject of conjecture,
but appear to be limited to Moscow-based members of the
Politburo most immediately concerned with foreign affairs.[8] At the
present time these would be:

M. S. Gorbachev	General Secretary, CPSU; commander in chief
E. A. Shevardnadze	Full member, Politburo; Foreign Minister
D. T. Yazov	Candidate member, Politburo; Defense Minister
V. M. Chebrikov	Candidate member, Politburo; chairman, KGB
L. N. Zaykov	Full member, Politburo; specialist in defense industry and economics
N. V. Talyzin	Candidate member, Politburo; chairman, Gosplan
N. I. Ryzhkov	Full member, Politburo; chairman, Council of Ministers

Marshal S. F. Akhromeyev, chief of the General Staff, serves as a
nonvoting executive secretary for the body (Scott 1983: 48).

The Soviet *Military Encyclopedic Dictionary* (*Voenny entsiklo-*

pedicheskii slovar') simply describes the Defense Council as "the highest organ for the direction of the defense of the country," notes that it is "organized" by the Presidium of the Supreme Soviet in accordance with the Soviet Constitution of 1977, and lists as one of its "prototypes" the World War II State Defense Committee.[9] These clues, however, are sufficient to begin an analysis of the contemporary structure of control. They confirm that it is to the State Defense Committee (GKO)—the center of Soviet power during the Great Patriotic War—to which one must turn.

The Stalinist GKO was established on June 30, 1941, a little over one week into the German invasion. It endured until September 4, 1945, and in that time it was the unequivocal center of power. Its decisions had the force of law. The scope of its authority included "the mobilization of all human, material and other resources of the state for the security needs of war" and "the leadership of all forms of conflict in war, including ideological, economic and diplomatic struggle."[10] Given Stalin's tendency to obscure the formal lines of authority prior to the war, the creation of the GKO is all the more breathtaking a transformation. Stalin held no official government position until May 1941, but by August he held all of the titles and offices necessary to directly oversee the war effort at several levels. In doing so he created a network of overlapping committees that serve as the foundation of the present system.[11]

In addition to Stalin, the 1941 GKO consisted of Molotov, Voroshilov, Beria, and Malenkov. These five men, with Stalin as Supreme Commander in Chief, mobilized and guided the Soviet war effort. All but Malenkov were full members of the Politburo (Malenkov was a candidate member), and although four new members were added to the GKO as the war progressed, at no time could any member of that body be considered essentially a professional soldier.

Since the war, all of these individuals have disappeared. Stalin died in 1953, and Beria was executed soon thereafter. The others were removed for "anti-party" activities in 1957. But the system of command they created has adapted and endured.

Of course, this has not been a linear process: the atomic missile "revolution in military affairs" at one time suggested—at least to Khrushchev—a clean break with the past. The first conference on the impact of nuclear weapons came the year after Stalin's death, and for twenty years—1953 to 1973—the General Staff Academy had no faculty of military history. The Strategic Rocket Forces, organized in 1959, became the leading service of the Soviet armed forces.

Even under Khrushchev, however, the immediate impact of nuclear missile weapons on the organization of the highest echelons of command was less significant. At the height of Khrushchev's "one-variant" approach to war, the Defense Council continued to operate, and there remained plans for a revived GKO in time of war. The first two editions of *Military Strategy* (1962, 1963) declared that "all leadership of the country and the Armed Forces during wartime" may involve "the possible organization of a higher agency of leadership" with "the same powers as the State Committee of Defense during the Great Patriotic War," which "will be headed by the First Secretary of the Central Committee of the head of government, to whom the functions of Supreme Commander in Chief may also be entrusted."[12] In contemporary conditions, as the Soviets have come to reaffirm multiple variants and political contexts for war, the need for such a body is greater than ever.

It seems likely that today's Defense Council stands ready to transform itself into a new GKO. In an emergency the formal organizational transformation might even be made retroactively, as the members of the Defense Council—led by the General Secretary in his role as commander in chief—function to provide leadership based upon the authority of their peacetime roles.

Wartime military decision making will be the official responsibility of the Supreme High Command (VGK), immediately under the GKO. The VGK exists in both peace and war, yet even so the direct organizational influence of the full VGK may be less than it first appears.[13] With a membership that overlaps that of the Main Military Council, a body of ninety or more senior officers (including the Collegium of the Ministry of Defense), the size of the VGK and the numerous other tasks assigned to its members suggest that it is too unwieldy for quick decisions. Soviet authors have also pointed out that the Main Military Council failed to provide timely leadership in the initial phases of the Great Patriotic War, and have suggested that reliance on a contemporary analogue is not an attractive option (Kunitskiy 1986: 36). Overall, it seems likely that the VGK is more of a coordinating body that will consider the means of implementing the resolutions of other authorities (Sadkliewicz 1982: 201).

The STAVKA, or General Headquarters, of the VGK (SVGK) will serve as the supreme operational command authority (Danilov 1987: 30; Erickson 1962: 598; Hines and Peterson 1986: 285). Subordinate to the Politburo and the State Defense Committee, in a general war the membership of the SVGK will also overlap somewhat with that of the GKO.[14] Chaired by the General Secretary (functioning in his role as commander in chief), its remaining members are selected from the Collegium of the Ministry of Defense and include the Minister of Defense, the chief of the General Staff, the commanders in chief of each of the armed services, and perhaps one or more additional deputy ministers.[15] Although the Collegium has at least twenty members, there is reason to believe that the number of members of STAVKA is never greater than eleven.[16]

Immediately below the SVGK, the General Staff serves as the primary "control organ of the Armed Forces," given the task of "operational planning of campaigns and operations" as well as the "construction, training, application, and security of the Armed Forces" in both peace and war.[17] As in the years immediately before the Great Patriotic War, part of the peacetime function of the General Staff is the preparation of armed forces development and operational plans, subject to review and approval by political authorities. During war the General Staff is the direct subordinate and "principal working organ" of the STAVKA of the Supreme High Command, engaged in the "strategic planning and leadership of the Armed Forces at the fronts." In this role it will have the authority to coordinate not only the actions of the various services at the fronts, but also those at the rear.[18]

The General Staff is a prime example of the role of unanticipated consequences in the development of the structure and process of command. Traditionally, the party has been sensitive to the potential for "Bonapartism," and distrusting of the kind of professional military cadre exemplified by a General Staff. At no time has the Soviet General Staff played a role in policy-making comparable to that of the German General Staff between 1880 and 1918. Preceded by the Red Army Staff in 1918, and reorganized by the Frunze reforms of 1924–25, the General Staff did not come into its own as a formal entity until 1935. Even with the formal authority granted prior to the Second World War, "the political position of the General Staff was still very fragile" (Rice 1987: 58).

From the formation of the Red Army Staff to the start of the Great Patriotic War, the average tenure of a chief of staff was less than four years (Bayer 1987: 231).

The creation of the Secretariat for the Council of Labor and Defense (the forerunner of the Defense Council) to parallel the General Staff was considered in 1924, only to be rejected on the grounds of military inefficiency (Rice 1987: 58). During the 1930s Stalin chose not to mirror the functions of the General Staff within the apparatus of the Central Committee, but efficiency was not the prime motive for his decision. Instead, he was motivated by a need for more immediate and personal means of control. The General Staff "became a pawn in Stalin's attempts to maintain control over the Red Army and to weaken Tukhachevskii's influence over it" (Bayer 1987: 179). So long as the chief of the General Staff remained a Stalin loyalist, the formal authority of the organization grew, but only the formal authority. With the death of Stalin, and particularly since the fall of Khrushchev, that authority has moved from formality to reality.

During the Great Patriotic War, the chief of the General Staff countersigned all military documents with Stalin (Meyer 1987: 519, note 134). Today, he continues to countersign each draft of peacetime orders and instructions from the Minister of Defense. In addition, he serves as a gatekeeper between the Defense Minister and other Deputy Ministers of Defense, and in all likelihood has a greater understanding of day-to-day problems and alternatives than does the Defense Minister himself (Sadkiewicz 1982: 203–4). His role as executive secretary of the Defense Council makes him a key representative of military interests and issues to the political elite, and a conduit for political concerns and directives to the military.

Between the highest levels of the military hierarchy—the General Staff and the SVGK—and the elements of a strategic direction, "intermediate organs" are likely to play a significant role. Special representatives of the SVGK and General Staff, as in the Second World War, will serve to coordinate the various operational directions of each strategic direction. For the most critical strategic axes, such organs have already been established. High Commands of Forces (HCOF), such as that for the Western Theater of Military Action (TVD), are in place with large supporting staffs.[19]

It is obvious that the Soviets take the problems of wartime

command very seriously. Just as Soviet strategy integrates the political and military functions of deterrence and war fighting into a single conceptual scheme, the Soviet state includes a system of interlocking political and military organs for the rapid command of all the social, economic, and military resources of the nation in time of war. That the structure of the Soviet state should correspond so closely to the mechanisms in place during the Second World War is not merely a coincidence, but the direct result of the experience of that war. As the state continues to adapt to current conditions, it is to that wartime structure—and the concepts embodied within that structure—that the state turns today. Given the trauma of the war, it would be remarkable if the state did anything else.

The Concept of Control

Objective structure and the structure of ideas are, in general, mutually reinforcing. In the case of the structure of command, the center of the structure of ideas is the Soviet concept of control. As discussed by Soviet specialists, troop control (*upravleniye voyskami*) is a concept with greater breadth than that of the American C3I. Troop control includes almost all the factors relating to the direction and effectiveness of forces in combat. The functions of a troop control system include receiving, collecting, studying, representing and analyzing data, making decisions, tasking subordinates with missions, planning combat operations, organizing and supporting coordination, "the organizational development of the Armed Forces," and "the training and indoctrination of personnel."[20]

The automation of decision and control systems has been a high Soviet priority for several years. As seen by Soviet specialists, the "revolution in military affairs" of the early 1960s was as much a revolution in cybernetics and control as it was a revolution in weapons and delivery systems. At that time, basic research began in the field of military cybernetics—the study of "the basic principles covering the control of forces and weapons in combat through the synthesis of the findings of general cybernetics and military science" (Grange 1984:93). By the late 1960s the field of military cybernetics was not merely making progress in systems theory, operations research, and the mathematical modeling of combat operations, but it was also beginning to be applied by commanders (Erickson 1984: 93). At the same time, technical progress has not been found to invalidate the principle that "troop control is in the first place the control of people" (Altukov 1984: 62).

At the level of the strategic leadership, this conception of control leads one to emphasize the importance of the political ends and the context of war (Hart 1984). Thus, to analyze the Soviet control system apart from an examination of particular political scenarios means missing some of the subtlety in Soviet thought. There are concerns common to all levels and scenarios of command, however. One is the importance of time as an essential measure of the effectiveness of control. Nuclear exchanges, for example, are discussed in terms of competing timelines, with each side attempting to take action quickly enough to take advantage of the control cycle time of the other side.[21]

A timely decision process requires a complex network of communications between elements of the strategic leadership, as well as between the strategic leadership and forces in the field. Communications between members of the GKO and the other elements of the strategic leadership are the responsibility of the KGB Special Signal Troops, which operates a secure telecommunications system with multiple nodes and means of transmission. The KGB-operated system includes several telephone and radio networks, and satellites, all of which are independent of the military communications system (Barron 1974: 88; Sadkiewicz 1982: 189).

Soviet planning appears to assume that these multiple channels will be necessary to reroute disrupted communications, much as the German invasion forced the General Staff to contact the fronts through naval and civilian networks:

> For the maintenance of stability and continuity of troop control, especially in conditions of military action with the use of nuclear weapons, the rapid restoration of disrupted control is of paramount importance. To create an utterly invulnerable system of control does not appear to be feasible, and thus commanders and staffs must always be prepared for the restoration of disrupted control in a short time and in all kinds of conditions. (Altukov 1984: 106)

To facilitate this end, alternate command posts exist for the GKO, SVGK, General Staff and armed services. Seventy-five command posts of varying hardness exist in the Moscow area alone. More than 1,500 shelters for some 110,000 key officials and personnel are believed to link the Soviet Union, as well as mobile command posts on trains, trucks, and aircraft (Meyer 1987:504). The strategic leadership is not absolutely invulnerable. It is dispersed and well protected, however.

Another means of protecting the strategic leadership is the use of tight communications security. This also has the bonus of promoting operational surprise. Prior to the counterattack at Stalingrad, for example, orders were transmitted from the SVGK orally, and only to officers with an immediate need to know (Kunitskiy 1987: 40). In a future war the possibility of a similar surprise should not be discounted.

Beyond the technical requirement to transmit orders to the forces in the field, it is equally necessary to ensure that the orders are carried out. This plus the Soviet emphasis on the political context for war provide a rationale for the elements of the Soviet military not found in the Western model. These range from the program of political indoctrination by the *zampolit* of the Main Political Administration to the monitoring of the military by the KGB. Indeed, given the number of Party members in the military— particularly in the higher echelons and throughout the strategic forces—the distinction between "Party" and "military" is some-times less than useful. Another example of the way in which the roles of the Party and military can interact is the important role political officers appear to have in the nuclear launch control process. It has been confirmed that Soviet regulations require a political officer to always be on duty in each ICBM launch control center.[22]

The Leadership Process

The process of command is reflected and shaped by the structure of command. Nothing short of putting the structure into operation, however, can resolve all of the uncertainties. No amount of preplanning can anticipate every consequence of the trans-formation of command.

Although the general course of the transformation from peacetime to wartime command is foreshadowed by the Soviet experience in the Great Patriotic War, a contemporary war would of course require much greater speed and flexibility. Soviet specialists recognize this need for rapid action, as is indicated by the growing evidence of more centralized preplanning for all Soviet strategic nuclear forces. The General Staff has been tasked to create—and in wartime, execute—a set of coordinated operational plans for the Strategic Rocket Forces (RVSN), navy, and air force similar to the American Single Integrated Operational Plan (SIOP).[23] If anything, history suggests that these plans may be even more integrated than the SIOP, given the traditional Soviet interest in combined arms operations.

For decades the Soviet strategic leadership has indicated a willingness to wait for an immediate threat prior to the transformation of the leadership structure. Unlike the United States, which appears to have a greater emphasis on tactical warning, Soviet strategic threat assessments rely as much on political and diplomatic indicators as on technical means (Meyer 1987:497–500). If triggered by a crisis, the expansion to the full wartime organizational structure can occur quickly, and with little outward evidence for the West (Deane et al. 1984:66–67).

This willingness to delay the transformation is not without some risk. It may be tolerated, however, because of a contradiction built into the Soviet state: the tension between collective decision making and one-man command.

In wartime, particularly if nuclear weapons are involved, the complexity and scope of combat operations is described by Soviet authors as making some form of collective leadership "an objective necessity" (Skirdo 1970: 146). In addition, of at least equal concern to the political elite in peacetime is the fact that a norm of collegiality has developed as a guiding principle in relations between senior officials in the years since the death of Stalin. The emphasis on maximizing consensus has been a matter of simple self-interest.

As a practical matter, however, command by consensus is not noted either for its efficiency or its brilliance. As a recent Soviet textbook on troop control observes,

The complex conditions of the preparation and conduct of modern operations, the vast and destructive force of weapons in use, the transience of the military actions of troops and the sharp changes of situation have significantly heightened the role of the time factor and the

necessity of accepting the individual decision and its firm execution in
life. This may only be found in the strict centralization of rights in the
hands of one person—the commander. (Altukov 1984: 58)

The Soviet military has long accepted the need for "one-man
command" (*edinonachalie*), involving clearly defined individual
areas of authority, and corresponding personal responsibility for
failure and success. The policy of *perestroika* has noted that
"personal responsibility" is a concern in the military and throughout the society, but in so doing it has reaffirmed a prior tenet of
Soviet military thought. The replacement of Defense Minister
Sokolov and Air Defense Marshal Koldunov with Dimitri Yazov
and Ivan Tretyak (immediately following the penetration of Soviet
air space by a West German Cessna on Air Defense Day) is an
example of the way in which the principle of one-man command
can be applied to even the most senior officers (Herspring 1987).
For the military, the tension between individual and collective
leadership is resolved by accepting that "one-man command and
collective leadership emerges in a dialectical unity in the leading
role of the commander. The commander in his work leans on
deputies, staffs, political and other organs of control. Together
with them he discusses the fundamental questions of the preparation
and conduct of operations" (Altukov 1984: 59). The commander,
however, does not share with subordinates the ultimate responsibility for the decision.
Another means of managing complexity is by producing, as
much as possible, "scientifically substantiated" methods and plans
in keeping with the principles of Soviet military science. Thus, as
Condoleezza Rice has pointed out, the primary beneficiaries of the
quest for "laws of war" have been the military professionals of the
General Staff (Rice 1987: 61).
How may this be applied to the more political roles of the
strategic leadership? At the highest level of the Party and
government the roles of superior and subordinate may often be
poorly defined. There is but one individual in the Defense Council
who is unquestionably the first among equals. In all situations, the
role of the General Secretary is critical. If a situation requires action
in a matter of minutes, that role is even more critical.
In the initial phase of a war, the Defense Council will transform
into the GKO. This should not require a week, as in 1941, but could

occur almost immediately as predelegated responsibilities and authority are attached to the roles of the general secretary and several of his predelegated Politburo associates. It is during the transition that the tension between collective decision making and one-man command may become most acute, particularly if the political indicators in a crisis remain ambiguous. A majority of the Politburo, however, and almost all the members involved in national security affairs are already functioning as members of the Defense Council. There is little reason to assume that the transformation from the Defense Council to the GKO could be delayed by internal dissent.

The process of decision making within the GKO is likely to depend upon both the issues to be resolved and the time available. In a crisis, the general secretary must be capable of responding to the improbable "bolt-out-of-the-blue." Like the American president, he remains within easy reach of the "football" containing the nuclear release codes (Meyer 1987: 484). In his response, he will in all likelihood depend on the advice and options presented by the military. The chief of the General Staff is in a position to have a very influential role at such a time.

As the time available for decision increases, so can the participation of the other members of the GKO. It is possible that this may broaden the information base without significantly altering the assumptions underlying strategic decisions. As they adapt to wartime contingencies, this highest level of the strategic leadership will define the objectives of the war, specify the means available for the achievement of those goals, and mobilize the full resources of the Soviet state. At this level, planning will concentrate on "an appraisal of the possible course of the war as a whole and the military actions on independent directions," as well as "the determination of strategic objectives and tasks." This appraisal will rely in part on an estimation of the correlation of forces, including not only military, but political, economic, and moral elements.

The Supreme High Command (VGK) will contribute to the formulation and implementation of policy. Its members' primary role, however, will involve the implementation of decisions made elsewhere. The STAVKA of the VGK (SVGK), however, will be in a position to immediately assume an active decision making role. With a membership that overlaps both the GKO and the General Staff, STAVKA is unavoidably at the center of military decision making.

Key decisions, as in World War II, are likely to run in parallel within the structure of the strategic leadership. During the war joint sessions of the Politburo, GKO, and SVGK reviewed enactments involving "the preparation and conduct of military campaigns and strategic operations," as well as "questions of the military-political situation of the country."[24]

These joint sessions may not involve assembling all the key decision makers in the same place. With the multiple communications networks of the military and KGB, it may not be necessary. However they are managed, they will select "the direction of the main strike in offensive operations," in order to maximize "important political, economic and strategic results." And, as in World War II, Soviet authors emphasize that the most important criteria for such decisions will be political (Kunitskii 1987: 30; Kulikov 1975: 18).

The General Staff, as the "principal working organ of the STAVKA," will expand its already considerable role in the direction and coordination of the activities of the armed services and the High Commands of Forces for the various Theaters of Military Action. Together with the STAVKA VGK, it will serve as the center for strategic planning, looking for the best means to obtain the goals specified by the GKO (Kulikov 1975: 18). Because of the rapid pace of battle, secondary tasks are likely to be delegated to others in order that the General Staff may concentrate on the direction of actions by the fronts (Kunitskii 1986: 36).

The General Staff will also manage the collection and evaluation of theater-level and strategic intelligence, including, for example, indicators of enemy preparations to employ nuclear weapons. These estimates will be provided to the SVGK (Meyer 1987: 515–16; Kulikov 1975:14). Of course, if nuclear weapons are employed, it is anticipated that the collection and evaluation of this critical information will be further complicated by the "grave losses" expected to be suffered by Soviet reconnaissance and intelligence means (Altukov 1984: 36). The parallel processing and multiple roles inherent in the Soviet command system, however, mean that the political leadership should always be at the center of the nuclear decision process.

At each level of the strategic leadership the structures refined and proven in the Second World War provide the foundation for action today: the Defense Council, the State Defense Committee, the

STAVKA VGK, and the General Staff each correspond to organizations found forty-five years ago. Current "organizational reforms," including the establishment of High Commands of Forces corresponding to critical Theaters of Military Action, continue to have one foot in the past.

Implications for the West

American scenarios for war with the Soviet Union are notorious for an air of unreality. There is always a temptation for an analyst to deny the importance of variables for which one has no firm measure. Soviet specialists, however, do not see war as unreal, nor does the Soviet approach to wartime decision making ignore the complexities of war. The Soviet state attempts to deal, as best it can, with both the technical and the human sides of war.

The loss of strategic superiority has prompted some in the West to search for weaknesses in the Soviet structure of command. This is an important task. Suggestions that the United States should plan to target the senior political leadership, and/or disrupt communications between the center and forces in the field, however, must take note of the difficulties and dangers of such a policy. The Soviet strategic leadership in wartime will be dispersed, shielded, and concealed. The military emphasizes the need for deputies and secondary centers to reconstitute disrupted mechanisms of control. It is true that for the political elite silence is the only visible response to the problem of succession. It is a substantial gamble, however, to assume that silence indicates a lack of preparation.

Soviet officers continually reevaluate the present and future in terms of the lessons of World War II, but this does not mean that the past serves as a "cookbook" for dealing with contemporary problems. As Marshal Tolubko, former chief of the Strategic Rocket Forces, recently observed,

> The creation of methods for the organization and maintenance of cooperation, demonstrated in the years of the Great Patriotic War, has not forfeited its significance in contemporary conditions. These relate first of all to the centralized coordination of the fundamental questions of cooperation by strategic organs of control with the assignment to initiatives of commanders and staffs, in the detailed work of interaction

in the execution of the main strikes, to the clear definition of missions
to troops and of the means of their decisions. . . . The study of this
experience and its creative application presents itself as an important task
of our military cadres. (Tolubko 1987: 19)

Those who are responsible for the direction of the Soviet military
in peace and war recognize that current problems require *creative*
action. They will not blindly mimic the solutions of the past. This
action, however, has occurred and will likely continue to control
Soviet military strategy within generally predictable limits. The
lessons of the Second World War have been internalized; Soviet
leaders generally accept that to ignore these lessons would be
inviting disaster. In its definition of the situation, its structure, and
its command process, the Soviet state continues to affirm the
experience of the war for the present day. No matter how the Soviet
state continues to evolve under Gorbachev, an appreciation of this
foundation is critical for an understanding of Soviet military affairs.

Notes

1   For a brief introduction to "statist" analysis, see Krasner 1984: 223–46 and
    Evans et al. 1985.
2   For an application of this approach to American foreign policy analysis, see
    Adelman 1986. An examination of the relationship between state structure and
    ideology can be found in Wuthnow 1985: 799–821.
3   Philip A. Bayer estimates that the Red Army lost over 70 percent of its officers
    during the Great Purge. See Bayer 1987: 179.
4   Marshal N. V. Ogarkov, "Pobedi i sovremenost [Victory and the Present
    Day]," *Krasnaya Zvezda* [Red Star] 9 May 1983, 2.
5   *Voenny entsiklopedicheskii slovar'* 1986: 711. For a similar distinction, see
    Altukov 1984: 57.
6   Michael Sadkiewicz has reported that he has found a Soviet reference that
    confirms the existence of the Defense Council in 1957. See Warner et al. 1987:
    4, footnote 2.
7   "Brezhnev," in *Voenny entsiklopedicheskii slovar'* 1986: 100.
8   A somewhat different estimate of the membership of the Defence Council can
    be obtained by generalizing from similar bodies in Eastern Europe. See Jones
    1985: 6–7.
9   "Council of Defense of the USSR," in *Voenny entsiklopedicheskii slovar'* 1986:
    684. The other prototype mentioned is the council of labor and defense, headed
    by Lenin, which operated during the Civil War.
10 "State Defense Committee," in *Voenny entsiklopedicheskii slovar'* 1986: 206
    and Kulikov 1975: 12.

11   Vernon Aspaturian, "The Stalinist Legacy in Soviet National Security Decisionmaking," in Valenta and Potter 1984.

12   Sokolovskii 1968: 361 and 461, editors note, 205. The third edition of *Military Strategy* dropped the reference to the role of the First Secretary.

13   For a reference to the existence of the VGK in peacetime, see Skirdo 1970: 136.

14   "Headquarters of the Supreme High Command," in *Voenny entsiklopedicheskii slovar'* 1986: 703.

15   Sadkiewicz 1982:199–200, and Stephen M. Meyer, "Soviet Nuclear Operations," in Carter et al. 1987:470–531.

16   Scott and Scott, 1983:50–51, suggest that there are six to eight members, with a "board of permanent advisors" overlapping Meyer's list.

17   "General Staff," in *Voenny entsiklopedicheskii slovar'* 1986: 185.

18   "General Staff," in *Voenny entsiklopedicheskii slovar'* 1986: 186.

19   Hines and Peterson 1986: 285. For examples from the Second World War, see Tolubko 1987.

20   Altukov, "Upravleniye voiskami," in *Sovetskaya voennaya entsiklopediya* 1980: 203. Quotes are taken from Gareyev 1985: 406.

21   Tarakanov 1974. An English translation of a key chart from this book can be found in Meyer 1987: 492.

22   A. Gorokov, "Za pul'tami strategicheskikh [At the strategic control panel]," *Pravda* 29 May 1985, 2.

23   Marshal N. V. Ogarkov, "Miru—nazdezhnuyu zashchitu [For Peace—A reliable defense]," *Krasnaya zvezda* 23 September 1983, 2.

24   "Headquarters of the Supreme High Command," in *Voenny entsiklopedicheskii slovar'* 1986: 703.

Part III

Implications for the Future

8

The Impact of World War II on Contemporary Soviet Military Theory

Notra Trulock III

The impact of the Great Patriotic War and World War II in general on contemporary Soviet military theory can hardly be overestimated. The evidence of this impact is immediately obvious in any Soviet military journal or Military Publishing House book addressing the problems and dilemmas confronting current military planners. It almost seems an unwritten rule that Soviet military theoreticians and authors must uncover suitable wartime examples or experiences in order to effectively convey the essence of their subject matter to the reader. Moreover, references to specific wartime examples in such publications are usually a reliable indicator of current analytical issues confronting these theoreticians. Soviet military literature is replete with such examples. To cite just a few, one could include analyses of wartime mobile groups and operations of groups at the front, as historical analogues for the Operational Maneuver Group and Strategic Operations in a Theater of Strategic Military Action (TVD). These historical analyses appeared at a time when Soviet military theory was elaborating the forms and methods of military operations made feasible by the integration of a new family of military technologies. The importance of such historical research has recently been underscored by a prominent

Soviet military historian, Lieutenant General M. M. Kir'yan. According to Kir'yan, "The contemporary views and theses of Soviet military theory rely on the richest historical experience, without which it would be impossible to comprehend the phenomena occurring in military affairs at the present time" (Kir'yan 1987: 3).

The Soviet military is understandably proud of the wartime achievements of its military theory and military art. Marshal S. Akhromeyev, the chief of the Soviet General Staff, has credited the superiority of Soviet military theory as being one of the most decisive factors in the Soviet victory in the Great Patriotic War (Akhromeyev 1985). The Soviets are not content to simply dwell on their past successes, however. They are determined that field commanders and their staffs learn from the mistakes and miscalculations of the past. Here too, the Soviet World War II experience offers a rich database of numerous examples and instances of how not to conduct military operations and strategic analysis. In this regard, the Soviet experience in the initial period of that war, and especially the events preceding June 1941, seem of special relevance to contemporary military analyses.

Lieutenant General V. Serebryannikov, for example, recently reminded his readers of the catastrophic consequences resulting from an overreliance on political measures at the expense of military vigilance prior to the outbreak of the Great Patriotic War (Serebryannikov 1987: 12). In a thinly veiled reference to the current discussion of political as opposed to military technical means as the best method to ensure national security, Serebryannikov warned of the negative effect on military vigilance of the frequent references in the Soviet media to progress on arms control and overly optimistic estimates of the future threat environment. Particularly telling was Serebryannikov's referral to the consequences of a similar media campaign prior to June 1941. Similarly, General Yu. Lebedev, a deputy chief of the General Staff's Treaty and Arms Control Directorate, has sought to justify sustained military spending through reference to the Soviet Union's Great Patriotic War experience. According to Lebedev, "we Soviets cannot repeat what happened in 1941. The defeat occurred because of a lack of attention to the Army's need, and there are still countries that consider us their enemy and that threaten us."[1]

Clearly, then, the Soviet experience in World War II serves a multitude of functions. There can be no question, however, that it has served as a rich source of inspiration and stimulation for the contemporary development of Soviet military theory.

This chapter is intended to portray some of the lessons the Soviet military have derived from their experience in the Great Patriotic War. A full treatment of all of the conclusions of contemporary Soviet military theory is beyond the scope of this chapter. Therefore, the focus is upon three specific themes. The first covers the relationship of the wartime experience to contemporary efforts to forecast the nature of future warfare. This is a subject of increasing importance to the Soviets as military affairs continue to evolve under the impact of an accelerated scientific-technical revolution. Second, the chapter traces the evolution of Soviet military theory on the potential inherent in the military systems that result from this scientific-technical revolution for fulfilling wartime strategic objectives without resorting to nuclear weapons. Finally, the chapter reviews the military planning requirements inherent in Soviet conclusions about the nature of future war for the strategic leadership of the armed forces and the country in such a war. This is a particularly critical subject for the Soviets since so much of the 1941 disaster may be traced to the failure to have a strategic leadership structure in place before the war. Such an oversight in the current period could have, according to the Soviet analysis, catastrophic consequences not only for Soviet military operations, but also for the continued existence of the Soviet state.

Soviet Strategic Analysis: The Relevance of the Wartime Experience

One of the key lessons the Soviets have learned from their Great Patriotic War experience regards the importance of timely and accurate strategic analysis of the evolving forms, methods, and means of modern warfare. The Soviet military has a vivid memory of the potential disasters that result from interruption of military forecasting of the future. Despite enormous progress in the development of both forces and operational concepts before the outbreak of the Great Patriotic War, the failure of the military leadership to "deeply analyze the character of war and the combat

potential of the probable enemy" cost the Soviet Union dearly
(Akhromeyev 1984: 23–24). Soviet failures in the early days of the
war can be explained, in part, by the intervention of the political
leadership into military preparations. It is equally clear, however,
that the Soviet military's plans simply did not correspond to the
realities of the warfare of that period. The military's key assumptions about the way the war would begin and the basic German
concepts of operations proved seriously mistaken. In particular,
the failure of both the Soviet political leadership and especially the
military leadership to comprehend the implications of earlier
German operations against Poland and in Western Europe proved
disastrous for the Soviet Union in June 1941. Soviet military
planners assumed that initial engagements would be fought with
limited forces in order to provide cover for full mobilization and
deployment. According to General Ivanov's account of these
events, "As the first days of the war showed, this assumption was
not justified" (Ivanov 1986: 176–77). For example, the Soviet
military failed to consider that German air forces would conduct
preemptive attacks on Soviet military airfields, an assumption that
cost the Soviets about 1,200 aircraft in the first days of the war.

In a major address to a military science conference devoted to an
investigation of the fundamental turning point of that war, Marshal
S. Akhromeyev warned that, "At the present time, our command
cadres must learn these lessons. It is necessary to remember that
changes in the character of war are now proceeding more rapidly,
and this means that our reaction to these changes, to the demands
of Soviet military art and to the development of the Armed Forces
must be more energetic."[2] The Soviets have come to realize that
nothing is immutable in the development of military affairs, least
of all military doctrine and military art. They believe that military
doctrine covers primarily the present period and the immediate
future and, under the impact of a number of factors, this doctrine
will eventually become outdated and in need of replacement
(Kozlov 1971: 65).

Through long experience and careful attention, the Soviets
believe they are well structured to undertake the difficult task of
forecasting alternative military futures. It is their view that military
science is the "science of future war" and that this science must
forecast not only the nature of such wars, but also the most effective
operational concepts and the main directions of force development

in order to conduct such wars. Beyond this, however, the Soviets believe this process must also be capable of forecasting alternative futures, both of a favorable and especially of an unfavorable nature. It is only through the latter approach that the political and military leadership can formulate strategies that will enable the Soviet Union to "shape the actual form of the operation of objective trends in more favorable directions" (Shavrov and Galkin 1977: 64).

Consequently, the Soviets have developed two levels of military forecasting. The first concentrates on the character of a war fought with extant military technologies and under the current correlation of forces of the sides. The second level is more oriented to the future and has three basic objectives:

1   It must identify the basic directions of military technical progress, the likely forms of the modernization of current systems and the appearance of qualitatively new military systems;
2   It must uncover the nature of further changes in force structure, the correlation of the arms of service, and the means of attack and defense; and,
3   It must identify potential problems associated with the increase of combat readiness of the forces necessitated by the character of future war.

The Soviets believe that the solution of these tasks is an absolute "prerequisite for long-range planning of the development of the armed forces" (Shavrov and Galkin 1977: 67).

Moreover, the Soviets place great emphasis on stability among the cadres oriented to military-scientific work and the availability of methodologies and techniques, which are considered to be most suitable to forecasting. For example, the application of dialectic laws drawn from historical materialism to military affairs prohibits the Soviet forecaster from an excessive reliance on simple-minded straight-line projections of force trends. Instead, it teaches him to look for critical nodes within these trend lines in which quantitative developments produce qualitative shifts.[3] Consequently, the Soviets have structured their assessment process to provide for the applications of these laws over the near term (about 5 years hence), the mid term (5–10 years in the future), and the long term (10 years and beyond) (Chuyev and Mikhailov 1975: 14).

In 1984 Colonel General M. A. Gareyev, then chief of the General Staff's Military Science Directorate and now a deputy chief, set forth a very concise statement of the tasks confronting contemporary Soviet military scientists. According to Gareyev, "military science must anticipate (in Russian, *predividet'*) the military-technical character of a possible war, its scale and the methods of the conduct of (strategic) military actions. It forecasts the trends in the development of military technology and, through this, in military affairs in general."[4] Implicit in this statement is the development of alternative scenarios for defense planning, strategies for the management of long-term research and design, and the formulation of Soviet responses and countermeasures to adverse developments in military technology and "military affairs in general." The emphasis on continually looking ahead in the attempt to predict and therefore avoid unfavorable circumstances clearly has its roots in the Soviet military's failure to anticipate the style of military operations that would characterize the conduct of the Great Patriotic War. For this reason, Soviet assessments of new defense technologies encompass not only the contribution of these technologies to current mission requirements, but also the potential impact of these technologies on the nature of warfare itself.

The Emergence of Conventional Preferences in Soviet Military Theory: The Relevance of the Wartime Experience

In fact, it was this continual need to look ahead at the future development of military affairs that has enabled the Soviets to maintain their military forces and military art abreast of contemporary requirements. The decade of the 1970s has witnessed a Soviet force modernization program of impressive magnitude and scope, which has encompassed practically every dimension of the Soviet force posture. As part of this force modernization cycle, in the mid–late 1970s the Soviets began to introduce new or newly modified operational concepts, such as the operational maneuver group concept, and also to implement a series of organizational and command and control modifications to the overall Soviet force structure, thus completing the full cycle of force development. In each case the Soviets drew heavily upon their experience with operational concepts and strategic leadership arrangements in the Great Patriotic War.

This cycle of force developments had its origins in a reevaluation of the nature of future war that probably was conducted in the mid-1960s within the Soviet General Staff. The General Staff's assessment of that period encompassed a broad range of factors, but undoubtedly took as its starting point a reevaluation of the role of nuclear weapons in future war. By 1962 or 1963 segments within the Soviet military had already expressed concern for the overemphasis on nuclear weapons during the Khrushchev intervention into the formulation of military strategy. In the aftermath of Khrushchev's removal, the reassertion of a balanced approach to force development became the first order of business for the Soviet military-scientific community. "After the October (1964) Plenum of the CC CPSU [Central Committee of the Communist Party of the Soviet Union], certain incorrect views within military-scientific circles connected with the overevaluation of the potential of the atomic weapon, its influence on the character of war, and the further development of the Armed Forces were overcome" (Tyushkevich 1978: 476).

The conclusions of this reevaluation shaped much of the agenda for Soviet force development over the next twenty years. Soviet military theory continued to be influenced, in part, by the growing skepticism over the feasibility of general nuclear warfare, at least as it had been envisioned in the earlier Soviet view of future war. This skepticism appears to have become especially pronounced not only within the political leadership, but also in the General Staff by 1971 or 1972 (Zemstov n.d.: 40–42).

The most critical event of this period, however, was the impending achievement of parity with the United States in terms of intercontinental ballistic missiles. Although most Soviet military sources retrospectively assess full achievement of strategic parity not to have occurred until about 1970 or 1971, it was probably evident to Soviet military planners of the mid-1960s that the fulfillment of this goal was in sight. The Soviet assessment of the consequences and implications of this achievement can hardly be overestimated. A 1972 Soviet analysis of the consequences of strategic parity for Soviet foreign policy, for example, concluded

The Soviet Union and other Socialist countries, by virtue of their increasing military potential, are changing the correlation of military forces in the international arena in favor of the forces of peace and socialism; this is having a sobering effect on the extremist circles of the imperialist states and is creating favorable conditions for the realization of Soviet foreign policy objectives in the world arena on the basis of the principles of peaceful coexistence. (Zulich 1972:222)

The military implications have been treated in considerable detail in Western sources and will not be discussed here. It is sufficient to note that both Soviet political and military leaders consider this event to be a, and perhaps even *the*, historic achievement of socialism.

This agenda was also shaped by the dilemma of how best to reduce the overreliance of Soviet planners on their own nuclear weapons. Soviet military planners of the mid-1960s concluded that both extant and near-term technologies afforded the opportunity —given the right conditions and skillful application—to achieve their strategic objectives without resorting to nuclear weapons. They believed that the correct application of these technologies, in mass, would increase the firepower and mobility of Soviet forces. Equally important, they believed that new control technologies would provide the capability to effectively manage, and thereby enhance the employment of these forces (Zhilin 1986: 400). In effect, the Soviets believed that the combination of massed, but controlled firepower and maneuver could substitute for the effects of nuclear strikes. The Soviets have never accepted the simple-minded assertion that such a substitution could somehow be accomplished on a one-for-one basis, nor do they assume such substitutions to be feasible even with the introduction of precision-guided munitions. Instead, the Soviets intended to substitute the concentrated and focused application of firepower and maneuver of several services and arms of service, in a combined-arms fashion, at the decisive places and times in any future conflict. These analytical assumptions were tested in a number of large-scale exercises in the late 1960s and were found to be valid (see, for example, Zheltov 1969).

Soviet analysis of future warfare was conducted, however, through reference to their wartime experience. In order to more effectively and systematically exploit this experience, in 1966 the Soviets established the Institute of Military History, which reports to the Ministry of Defense. The institute's primary purpose seems to be the identification and analysis of specific military history with "current applied significance" (Zhilin and Tinin 1985: 5). The institute probably works closely with the General Staff's Directorate of Military Science in the development of historical databases, and so on, for operational analyses of contemporary problems. Recent publications of the institute have focused upon the Soviet historical experience in relation to such current problems of Soviet military theory as strategic encirclement, surprise in offensive operations, and wartime front offensive operations. Many of the principles underlying the development of their military art were validated through the analysis of examples from the previous war. Soviet military theoreticians during the Khrushchev intervention into military affairs had argued that many of the theses of Soviet military theory had become outmoded and that the wartime experience had little relevance to contemporary warfare. As the Soviets began to move away from a reliance on nuclear weapons, they apparently realized that they were badly in need of a database replete with examples of different variants of the conduct of conventional operations.

Consequently, the Soviets concluded that the impact of these technologies on future theater war was to be manifested through an increase in both the potential scale of nonnuclear operations and the potential intensity of this conflict. With regard to the latter, the Soviets believed that future nonnuclear conflicts would be characterized by the intense struggle to seize the initiative, to impose one's will on the opponent, and to dictate the contours of the conflict. A key objective would be to continuously keep an opponent off-balance through the selection of unanticipated methods of fire and maneuver.[5] The Soviets believed that it should be possible to conduct decisive operations from the very beginning of such a conflict, but they also expected rapid and even unanticipated changes to occur at all levels of warfare. Consequently, they increasingly emphasized the necessity for continuous, uninterrupted operations regardless of weather, night, nuclear or nonnuclear conditions.

In response to the increasing scale of future operations, the Soviets returned to the concept of a strategic operation in a continental Theater of Strategic Military Action (TVD) that would coordinate the activities of a number of Soviet fronts as a substitute for the single front exploitation of nuclear strikes envisioned in the

1960s.[6] The best historical precedent for this strategic operation was considered by the Soviets to be their experience with "operations of groups of fronts" during the war. The key components of such a future strategic operation would be the air operation, frontal forces operations, air defense operations, assault operations, and, along littoral areas, the naval operations. The air operation and air defense operations were considered essential to the overall success of the strategic operation (Zhilin 1986). Each such operation would have its own objectives, timelines, and specific methods, but each would be conducted according to a unified plan and concept and under the overall control of a unified commander. A primary difference between the wartime operations of groups of fronts and future strategic operations, according to the Soviets, was that future strategic operations would be conducted without pauses, as were operations of the groups of fronts during the war. The Soviets seemed to realize that rapid achievement of their strategic objectives would necessitate continuous operations in order to prevent the enemy from regrouping his forces, bringing his enormous economic potential to bear on wartime operations, or considering escalation alternatives. It is important to recognize, however, that the Soviets realized that the conventional capabilities of that period meant that operational and strategic objectives could only be achieved in a sequential fashion, rather than simultaneously as during the nuclear emphasis period.

In order to execute such operations, the Soviets undertook a series of forces modernization programs, the results of which are generally known in the West. By the mid-1970s Soviet military specialists believed that the Soviet approach, which emphasized initially quantitative and later qualitative dimensions of force development, had provided the Soviet Union with a margin of military-technical superiority over the West. This margin of superiority had been obtained through a period of sustained growth in procurement of all forces at rates of four percent to five percent yearly, until about 1976. After this date, although strategic offensive and defensive forces experienced a reduction in real growth, nonnuclear forces procurement continued to grow, albeit at a slower rate of about 1.5 percent yearly (*Allocation* 1984: 14). The tactical-technical characteristics of newer generations of Soviet weapons have consistently featured greater range, improved lethality, more flexibility, and better responsiveness and reaction times in comparison with their predecessors. The integation of these systems into Soviet units has necessitated considerable midcourse experimentation and modifications to both organizational structures and employment methods. The means called upon to support the execution of air operations, for example, have expanded to include conventionally armed tactical ballistic missiles. The planning for Soviet front and army operations continues to experiment with the employment of operational maneuver groups and vertical assault operations. Many of the fundamental conclusions and patterns of employment of these concepts were developed through reference to the Soviet wartime experience.

Soviet ground force structures, especially the groups of forces deployed in Eastern Europe, have been in a continual process of change since the early 1970s.[7] Soviet divisions in these areas have experienced significant improvements in mobility and, in particular, firepower. These divisions continue to be held at the highest peacetime readiness standard with the overall effect of producing, in both motorized rifle and tank divisions, a better balance of fire and maneuver capabilities. Logistic and material support to these forces have undergone similar improvements, as have non-divisional (front and army) fire and maneuver elements. The overall intent of these modernization and organizational efforts has been to field a force structure capable of "conducting combat operations both with the use of nuclear weapons and with the use of only conventional means"(Kir'yan 1982: 326). Most Soviet military spokesmen of the period agreed that both force developments and military science were "completely answering those requirements presented by contemporary war to the armed forces" (Sorokin 1978:89).

In fact, Marshal Ogarkov's 1979 entry on military strategy in the *Soviet Military Encyclopedia* is indicative of just how far the Soviets had moved away from the 1960s mass nuclear employment scenarios and pessimism over the ability to control escalation. According to Ogarkov,

> Soviet military strategy assumes that world war may begin and continue for a certain time with the use of only conventional weapons. However, the expansion of strategic military actions *may* lead to its transformation into a general nuclear war, the main means for the conduct of which will be strategic nuclear weapons.[8]

By 1982 the Soviet political leadership seemed sufficiently confident that the nuclear threshold of a future war had been raised to the point that it would authorize the inclusion of a similar formulation in statements of military doctrine. Military doctrine, by definition, represents the Party's guidance to the military on such subjects as the nature of future war, the probable enemy (enemies), and the military-technical tasks of the armed forces, which includes the methods of conducting such a war.

According to a statement of the conclusions of military doctrine published that year, "a future war may be unleashed with either conventional or nuclear weapons; having begun with the use of conventional weapons it *may* at a definite stage be transformed into a nuclear war (Kir'yan 1982: 312). The author of this statement, a prominent military historian, went on to assert, "The successes of the Soviet Union in the area of military technology and weapons have convinced the imperialist strategists both of the doubtfulness of their concept of the shattering destruction of the USSR by means of a surprise massive nuclear strike and of the inevitability of retaliation" (Kir'yan 1982: 313). From this it is evident that by the early 1980s, both the Soviet military and political leadership had concluded that the only thing inevitable about the introduction of nuclear weapons into a conflict was the inevitability of retaliatory strikes in response to an attempted surprise first strike. These formulations of both military strategy and military doctrine seemed to reflect a Soviet conclusion that the threshold of nuclear use in a future conflict was likely to be quite high and perhaps might never be reached at all.

The Soviets clearly believe that nuclear weapons will continue to play an important, but gradually diminishing role in the further development of military theory. Nuclear weapons are likely, however, to continue to shape the operational context for military operations in the event of a future war. Deputy commander in chief for Combat Training of the Soviet Ground Forces Colonel General Merimskii has noted that the presence of nuclear weapons will continue to impose unique requirements on military planning (Merimskii 1984: 8). Soviet commanders will continue to address the dilemmas associated with the need, on the one hand, to disperse en route to commitment positions, so as not to present nuclear-suitable targets, but at the same time concentrate forces at decisive places and times to ensure success. Obviously, denuclearization of

NATO and Warsaw Pact force postures will alleviate these operational dilemmas somewhat. Not surprisingly, therefore, Defense Minister Yazov has graciously declared Soviet willingness to restructure Warsaw Pact forces along "non-nuclear principles" (Yazov 1987: 34).

From this and other Soviet statements, some in the West have concluded that the Soviet military now sees little, if any, military utility for nuclear weapons. This observation seems to ignore several key conclusions derived from Soviet military theory. First, as noted by Colonel General Merimskii, the mere existence of nuclear weapons imposes certain constraints and requirements on military planning. More importantly, however, the Soviets believe that the existence of an effective and survivable nuclear force could potentially deter an opponent from punishing Soviet aggression through nuclear attacks on the Soviet homeland. The capability to deter such attacks by the threat of assured retaliation represents a critically important function for Soviet strategic nuclear forces. Equally important, the existence of secure and effective theater nuclear forces, and especially the threat that such a force will be used in an irrational manner, could deter an opponent from using his nuclear weapons to deny achievement of the objectives of Soviet aggression. Consequently, the continued existence of such nuclear forces has a very real military utility in the sense that the intrawar deterrent inherent in such a capability could enable the Soviets to execute their concepts of a nonnuclear strategic operation unimpeded by an opponent's nuclear attacks. The Soviets clearly believe, however, that in order to fulfill such a deterrent role these forces must be both useable and effective; this conclusion was reached in the aftermath of the Khrushchev period and continues to represent Soviet military theory today.

Beyond this, however, the military may prefer to prepare and posture for a prolonged conventional war rather than rely on an "easy" resort to even precision-guided, low-yield nuclear attacks. This choice has been presented in stark terms in a number of recent authoritative statements by senior Soviet authorities. According to Marshal Akhromeyev's May 9, 1987 Victory Day article in *Red Star*, "Nuclear war may bring mankind to its grave. A world war with the use of conventional weapons, if it is unleashed by the aggressor, may also bring to mankind innumerable and even unforeseen disasters and suffering."[9] So, too, did World War II, but mankind survived that experience. Presented with such a dilemma, it seems evident that Akhromeyev's choice would be clear.

In 1988 the Soviets modified this choice somewhat by including references to nonnuclear attacks on nuclear power stations and chemical production facilities as having the potential for, in the words of Defense Minister Yazov, "catastrophic consequences comparable with a nuclear cataclysm."[10] Akhromeyev's discussion of the same issue was somewhat more temperate. He concludes only that "the likelihood of the deliberate destruction of nuclear power facilities and chemically dangerous production units will give such a war a destructive character not only regarding armies and navies, but also to the peoples of all continents.[11] The Soviets, of course, have very powerful incentives to deter enemy attacks against these facilities. There is, however, nothing in these statements to indicate that such attacks are somehow tantamount to crossing the nuclear threshold. In fact, Akhromeyev makes explicit this view by going on to state that in a conventional war "it must be also taken into account that such a war could at any moment turn into a nuclear war" (1987: 2). It is only the inclusion of these targets, however, that threatens consequences even remotely comparable to general nuclear war. Further, there appears to be an interesting correlation between Soviet references to the dangers of conventional attacks on such facilities and the rationale offered by Western European opposition parties for the removal of US nuclear weapons from Europe.

This choice may also reflect the essence of Marshal Ogarkov's message to both his internal military critics and the Party leadership. Ogarkov clearly believed it is far better to prepare for a prolonged, intensive and bitter, but nonnuclear struggle, than to count on some easy solution to be achieved through nuclear attacks. Soviet confidence in either side's capability to execute a disarming first strike, for example, has been waning for years and now seems at an all-time low. According to the Soviet analysis, both sides have sufficient diversity and protection for strategic nuclear forces to ensure the execution of a retaliatory strike that would, in Ogarkov's view, "even with the limited number of nuclear weapons remaining to the defender, deprive the aggressor of the potential afterwards to conduct not only the war, but also any type of serious operations . . ." (Ogarkov 1985: 89). Ogarkov's curious reference to "not only the war, but also . . . serious operations" apparently refers to retaliatory strikes against not only military forces in the field, but also the set of war-supporting targets in the homelands. Although ostensibly directed to a Western audience, there should be little doubt that the intended recipients of his message are key decisionmakers within the Soviet elite. Better to expend precious resources on nonnuclear forces, especially those forces with a potential for military effectiveness that approaches that of the weapons of mass destruction, than to risk the catastrophic consequences inherent in reliance on nuclear forces.

Consequently, for both military and political reasons there would appear to be little support for the proposition that new conventional weapons, at least in the Soviet perspective, would lower the nuclear threshold of a major conflict. Instead, the Soviets seem to believe that with less need to resort to these weapons to solve military problems, the threshold should be pushed progressively higher. Moreover, Soviet military leaders seem to prefer prolonging conventional operations rather than resorting to nuclear weapons in the event of a stalemated offensive. Obviously, such a conclusion also supports their claim for continued access to their traditional share of resources, but also probably reflects a genuine desire to avoid both the risks and complexities of operations in a nuclear environment.

The Implications of Soviet Perceptions of Future Warfare

The implications of Soviet conclusions with regard to the potential nature of future war have raised an additional set of analytic requirements for Soviet military theory. These have included the mobilizational and economic requirements required to sustain prolonged conventional operations, the reintroduction and reinterpretation of strategic principles for military planning, which had been discarded in the early 1960s, and the set of requirements associated with the strategic leadership of such operations.

With regard to the necessity to prepare for sustained conflict, the Soviets believe that they need to prepare for a prolonged conflict, regardless of whether this conflict is fought with nuclear or conventional weapons. They have explicitly stated their conclusion that a "future nuclear world will not be concluded rapidly," and Soviet preparations for this eventuality are generally recognized in the West (Zhilin 1986: 107). Although they hope to avoid protracted nuclear operations through a rapid and decisive nonnuclear victory, they also appreciate that the introduction of new conventional systems could reduce the likelihood of such an outcome. "In these conditions, as it is believed in the West, the potential for the conduct of a comparatively long war with the use of conventional weapons, especially new types of high-accuracy weapons, is increasing" (Gareyev 1985: 240). Soviet military theoreticians appear to generally agree with this judgment. They believe that regardless of whether a war is fought with nuclear weapons or conventional systems only such wars would be protracted because of the huge military and economic potentials of the opposing coalitions (Kir'yan 1982: 314). The notion that the Soviets would only contemplate short war, quick victory scenarios also colors much of Western thinking on this subject. No one could deny that the Soviets would seek such an outcome, but the Soviets seem to believe that it is naive to think that such an outcome would be easily achievable. General Gareyev made this point very effectively in 1985.

> In contemporary conditions the outcome of war to a significantly greater degree than before depends on the quality and effectiveness of the efforts put forth at the very beginning of the war; however, the strategic principle of the *economy of forces* has in general been preserved in as much as in a war between large coalitions with enormous potential capabilities it would be difficult to count on its swiftness (of conclusion). It is therefore necessary to be prepared for a long, stubborn, and bitter armed conflict. (Gareyev's emphasis)

Soviet military scientists appear to see no contradiction between this conclusion and the likelihood that these systems would increase the tempo of conventional operations dramatically. They apparently have concluded that the combination of anticipated attrition, interdiction of forward-deploying forces, disruption of control, and simply the increased complexity of operations inherent in the introduction of these systems would force a consideration of prolonged operations. Although the evidence is fragmentary, it appears that the Soviets are planning for a war of at least one year's duration.[12]

Such a conclusion has enormous implications for strategic leadership arrangements. In fact, Soviet strategic leadership requirements have received considerable attention in Soviet military leadership since the mid-1960s. Much of the attention at that time was generated by the dissatisfaction among Soviet military theoreticians with the current arrangements for the wartime leadership structure. The structure of wartime strategic leadership may also have become one of the key topics of contention in the post-Khrushchev development of political relationships. The conflict between the political leadership and the senior military authorities may have been largely resolved by the mid-1970s. However, a compromise was involved. The precise nature of this compromise is unclear, but it apparently left many of the details of security planning, in the words of then Premier Kosygin, "to the marshals" (cited in Wolfe 1975: 15).

This compromise failed to resolve fully the issue of wartime strategic leadership requirements, however. Soviet military sources continued to devote a significant degree of attention to the manner in which senior political and military authorities would manage both the armed forces and the country in general in the event of a major war. Moreover, it became increasingly evident that evolving Soviet views on strategic leadership were being heavily influenced by changing Soviet conclusions on the nature of future wars.

Since about 1965, Soviet military scientists have sought to keep pace with the changing forms and methods for conducting warfare that were created by the rapid development of technology, the changing nature of the "threat," and the increasing scope of Soviet foreign commitments. The evolution of Soviet views on these topics has led to the creation of a new set of tasks for wartime strategic leadership. Much of the research underlying these tasks was performed in connection with Soviet investigations of the initial period of war. Soviet attention to the initial period originated in the mid-1950s with the acceptance of the increased role of surprise in warfare, but was intensified in the late 1960s. According to the then Commandant of the Voroshilov General Staff Academy, Army General Ivanov, the academy undertook a major research project on the initial period with the instruction of the Soviet Minister of Defense (Ivanov 1971: 42). The product of this research was documented in a series of articles in the Soviet General Staff journal, *Voyennaya Mysl'*, in the early 1970s and in a book-length treatment in 1974 (Ivanov 1971: 42). The study noted the increasing importance of the role of surprise, the trend toward the prepositioning of large force groupings capable of initiating significant military operations at the very beginning of a war without a prolonged period of mobilization, and at least the potential for creating the conditions in the initial period for a victorious conclusion to the war. The integration of strategic and theater nuclear weapons into the forces of both major alliances served to underscore for the Soviets the importance of an accurate estimation of the nature of the initial period of war.

A combination of factors converged in the mid-1980s, however, to apparently force the Soviets to revisit the issue of the initial period of war. First, the Soviets professed to see an increasing aggressiveness on the part of the Western alliance and especially the United States. They continued to assert that a massive, disarming first nuclear strike remained the preferred U.S. approach to initiating combat operations and pointed to the U.S. strategic offensive forces' modernization efforts, especially those associated with the development of prompt hard-target kill capabilities, as evidence of U.S. intentions. Although the propaganda value of such assessments is obvious, prudent military planners could not fail to continue to consider such scenarios. Soviet military theoreticians continued to remind their readers that "first massive nuclear strikes are able in large measure to predetermine the entire course of the war and to bring about such losses in the rear and in the forces that could place the people and the country in an exceptionally difficult position" (Evseyev 1985: 16). There was little to distinguish this 1985 conclusion, however, from Soviet perceptions of the threat of strategic nuclear strikes in the early 1960s.

The Soviets appear more concerned with the potential of new nonnuclear systems to replicate the impact of strategic nuclear forces on the initial period of war. The Soviets repeatedly refer to the "rapid-action" and the range of these new systems for creating similar difficulties for the defender. In a 1985 analysis of the initial period of war, for example, Lieutenant General Evseyev concluded that "even when war begins with the use of conventional means, which possess large destructive force and significant range of operations, and also airmobile form and powerful armored means, the initial period could exert a huge influence on the consequent course of the war" (Evseyev 1985: 16). The Soviets pointed, in particular, to U.S. theater doctrinal developments as evidence of U.S. incentives to preemptively attack targets on Warsaw Pact and even Soviet territory with little or no strategic warning. According to these analyses, AirLand Battle, for example, "envisions the surprise initiation of military actions with the newest means of maximum destruction of the enemy and the conduct of decisive actions by ground, air, and naval forces to a depth, simultaneously enveloping the territory of an entire country" (Evseyev 1985: 16). The main conclusion of these studies conducted in the mid-1980s was provided by Lieutenant General Evseyev's analysis. According to Evseyev,

> The main content of the initial period of war in contemporary conditions may be the conduct by the opposing sides of nuclear strikes or strikes with the use of conventional means and, from the very beginning, active military operations by forces deployed in strategic groupings in peacetime for the achievement of the main goals of the war. Mobilization, deployment of armed forces to the TSMAs and the transition of the economy to a wartime status will be completed simultaneously. (Evseyev 1985: 16)

Accompanying this research was the reintroduction of the concept of the "threatening period." This, in turn, brought renewed attention to analysis of strategic warning indicators. During the early 1960s, Soviet military scientists believed that "War will begin suddenly and will demand the rapid introduction in the very first minutes of all the basic forces and means of armed conflict" (Kozlov 1964: 344). Such a war would have begun without a threatening period. There would be little time for mobilization. Soviet military scientists of that period anticipated a short war and, consequently, the wartime strategic leadership requirements would be minimal. Soviet military theoreticians of the period apparently believed that a well-developed plan and the forces and alert facilities necessary for its execution would satisfy these requirements.

By 1969, however, the concept of a threatening period had been reintroduced into Soviet military theory. This was connected, in part, with the adoption of a war-by-stages approach that envisioned a conventional stage of conflict preceding the escalation to nuclear use in the event of a major war. A conventional stage of war, in turn, created the requirement for the "preliminary deployment of strike groupings of troops in the zones of planned strikes and the conduct of a number of other preparatory measures . . . required for such operations" (Zemskov 1969: 45). As a result, the assessment of strategic warning indicators took on a somewhat different context in Soviet military theory. "A very deep evaluation of the developing situation and immediate reaction to measures and operations of the enemy will be necessary. The main thing here is not to be late or rule out surprise and not to give the enemy any advantages in developing the readiness of his armed forces" (Zemskov 1969: 46). Although Soviety military theoreticians acknowledged that it was the responsibility of the political leadership to determine an opponent's intentions and "immediate preparations for attack," the military reserved for itself the right to determine the beginning of the threatening period. "Under present day conditions one of the most important tasks of the military leaders is the timely determination of the onset of the period of threat immediately preceding the outbreak of hostilities and an enemy nuclear missile attack. . . . It is the task of the military leaders to detect these preparations in time" (Skirdo 1970: 116). Probably as a result of their analysis of the experience of the Great Patriotic War, the military leadership was apparently unwilling to abdicate completely their responsibility for determining the potential onset of hostilities.

The adoption of the war-by-stages concept dramatically increased the problem of ensuring continued political control over Soviet nuclear forces. There can be little doubt that these forces have always been tightly controlled by the political authorities. As a prominent Soviet military historian recently stated, "The fact of the matter is that the most powerful means of destruction—nuclear weapons—have been taken under control by the political leadership from the first days of their appearance" (Kir'yan 1985: 62).

Since the late 1960s, in particular, Soviet military sources have featured repeated references to political control over nuclear weapons. A General Staff Academy instructor, Colonel Skirdo, in his study of the role of strategic leadership in modern war, stated categorically, "The decision on the employment of such devastating weapons as nuclear weapons has become the exclusive prerogative of the political leadership" (Skirdo 1970: 116).

More recently, the Soviet no-first-use declaration seems to have increased Soviet concern over unauthorized release and use of nuclear weapons and led to Soviet efforts to further tighten control over these systems. In 1982 Marshal Ustinov, former Minister of Defense, called attention to the requirements for "still tighter control that will make sure an unauthorized launch of nuclear weapons, from tactical to the strategic level, is ruled out."[13] All this serves to indicate both the importance of this issue and the potential burdens on the Soviet decision-making structure to ensure such positive control.

Scenarios that featured the immediate employment of the entire arsenal of nuclear weapons would seem to require little in the way of extended control over nuclear forces. Such a requirement, however, would seem inherent in scenarios that feature conventional operations prior to escalation to nuclear employment. Moreover, in such scenarios, Soviet leaders would be faced with the task of ensuring the responsiveness of nuclear forces should the need arise to use these forces. Given the Soviet stress on positive, political control of nuclear forces in the context of conventional operations conducted under the constant threat of escalation, it seems clear that the decision to accept a conventional phase of conflict complicated the tasks of strategic leadership enormously.

Closely connected to this issue is the problem associated with determining the nuclear transition points within a conflict. As noted above, the Soviet military leadership has reserved to itself the role of detecting preparations for enemy nuclear use. Considerable attention has been devoted to the analysis of indicators of impending enemy use.[14]

Despite these efforts, the Soviets continue to be concerned over their ability either to forecast or to detect indications of transition points in a conflict. The problem apparently received considerable attention in the late 1960s, but by 1970 Lieutenant General Zav'yalov could only conclude that "[t]he complexity lies in the fact that it is difficult to foresee at what stage of the operation nuclear weapons may be employed" (Zav'yalov 1970: 211). Soviet investigations took a number of different approaches including the identification of "critical moments" within a conflict at which an opponent would have great incentives to introduce nuclear weapons. The Soviet leadership would likely have powerful disincentives to rely upon such a "templating" approach, however, and instead probably focuses upon developing estimates of the enemy situation based upon continuous streams of information. It is evident from this, however, that the decision requirements on the strategic leadership have expanded.

Changing Soviet views on future warfare have also had enormous implications for the mobilization of the country for wartime. The predominant view in the early 1960s held that mobilization would be impossible after the war was underway. War would be fought with existing forces, both sides would quickly expend their arsenals of nuclear weapons, and as a result wars would undoubtedly be short. Although the 1963 edition of *Military Strategy* identified the need to prepare for a long war, it is clear that the Soviets believed that in a major conflict with the West strategic objectives would be achieved quickly. Interestingly, the Soviets believed at that time that only poor strategic planning or a poorly executed plan would result in a protracted war (Kozlov 1964: 344).

These views have undergone considerable transformation. Most significantly, Marshal Ogarkov in his 1979 entry on "Military Strategy" in the *Soviet Military Encyclopedia* acknowledged that a future war could be of extended duration as a result of the huge military and economic potential of the opposing coalitions.[15] Marshal Ogarkov discussed this subject in further detail in his 1982 pamphlet, *Always in Readiness for Defense of the Homeland*. He noted the difficulties associated with the peacetime maintenance of forces at the level required by wartime operations (Ogarkov 1982: 58). As a partial solution, Ogarkov proposed that measures be established in peacetime that would ensure a smooth transition from peace to war. These would encompass not only the mobilization of reserves but also the transition of the peacetime economy to a wartime footing. According to Ogarkov, "The success of the organized entry of the armed forces into the war and the destruction of the aggressor depend largely on the complete and qualitative fulfillment of all these measures" (Ogarkov 1982: 60). In particular, Ogarkov identified the establishment of the wartime structure of strategic leadership as a critical factor in the successful mobilization of the country for war.

The combination of these factors with the changing Soviet views on the potential scope and scale of modern warfare, in turn, served to intensify Soviet interest in the role and function of strategic leadership. During the Khrushchev period, the subject apparently received some attention as both the 1962 and 1963 editions of *Military Strategy* provided an assessment of future wartime leadership arrangements. According to these accounts, an organization like the State Defense Committee of the Great

Patriotic War, headed by a supreme commander in chief, would be established to direct the Soviet war effort. Likewise, a Soviet Supreme High Command would be established to provide direct leadership of the armed forces (Sokolovskii 1963: 474).

The implication of this discussion was that such arrangements were not in place at that time but instead would be established before the initiation or at the outset of hostilities. By the late 1960s it was evident that Soviet military theoreticians were becoming uneasy over the status of preparations for wartime leadership. One indicator of this uneasiness was the increasing attention to their experience in the Great Patriotic War and especially the consequences of not having a leadership structure in place at the beginning of that war. For example, wartime Commander in Chief of the Soviet Navy Admiral Kuznetsov, reported in 1966, "Before the war, neither military institutions nor high defense officials had clearly defined rights and obligations. Experience has shown that in questions of supreme importance, the smallest ambiguity is intolerable. The war caught us without a properly prepared organization of the highest military leadership."[16] Kuznetsov's conclusion was that as a result, "We paid long and heavily for our poor organizational preparation."[17]

The lessons of that experience were clearly not lost on the Soviets. References in Soviet sources from the late 1960s would appear to indicate that arrangements for wartime leadership were undergoing intensive review and development during that period. Major General Zemstov, writing in 1967, indicated, "The necessary military-political organs for direction of the country and the armed forces in the event of war are already being created."[18] The clearest indication that such arrangements were not yet completed, however, was provided by General Zav'yalov in March 1967. Zav'yalov, in the context of a discussion of the doctrinal view of the question of wartime leadership, concluded, "The doctrine stresses that in modern war the unity of political and military leadership is necessary, and that sort of a collective agency is necessary which would manage to unite all the efforts of the state and direct them toward the achievement of the established goals."[19] These and other sources indicate both a dissatisfaction with current arrangements and the existence of an ongoing search for the correct forms and functions of wartime leadership in light of the changing objective conditions.

There are some indications in both the Western media and the Soviet press that the Soviet General Staff may have been intended to assume the role of a STAVKA of the Supreme High Command at this time. Hints of political dissatisfaction with this arrangement were expressed in a 1967 *Red Star* article. "The political leadership is also forced to inquire more actively and to a large degree into the solution of strictly military problems."[20] Some time later, such a role for the General Staff was publicly rejected, however, by the then chief of the General Staff, Army General (later Marshal) Kulikov.[21] In addition to the apparent absence of a strategic leadership organization, there were also indications of Soviet uneasiness over the lack of a military-economic organ to direct military development.

It seems evident from all this, therefore, that up to the mid-1960s the Soviets had given little thought to the subject of wartime strategic leadership, especially in the event of a prolonged conflict. To offset this glaring shortfall in their preparations for future war, Soviet military theoreticians undertook an intensive search for the correct wartime leadership arrangements. The Soviet research agenda appears to have been structured along the following lines. Considerable attention was devoted to contemporary arrangements in the West with frequent references to the "defense councils" of the United States, France, and the Federal Republic of Germany.

Soviet military leadership, however, reflected a more intensive interest in the historical experience with strategic leadership. This attention was by no means limited simply to the Soviet experience but encompassed also Allied and even Axis leadership structures. Moreover, attention was directed to the prewar experience of the Council of Workers and Peasants Defense and the Main Military Council as well.

Not surprisingly, however, the best model was considered to be the Soviet Great Patriotic War experience. Soviet assessments took as their starting points those features of the war experience that were similar to their projections of future war. In particular, the Soviets stressed the following characteristics of the Great Patriotic War as making that war relevant to a study of modern leadership requirements.

- The global scale of the war
- The dynamic, rapidly changing situations

- The war's coalitional nature
- The war's protracted character

The threat of nuclear war only intensified these considerations, which would be equally valid for a global conventional war. The Soviets appeared to believe that the scope of devastation and especially of the disorganization of control in the initial period of any future war could hardly be more extensive than that suffered early in the Great Patriotic War.

Soviet military theoreticians have continued to assert both the validity and utility of the wartime strategic leadership model. As recently as 1985, for example, General Mayorov, concluded, "The experience of the strategic direction of the armed forces, accummulated in the years of the Great Patriotic War, has largely preserved its significance in contemporary conditions. Its deep study, and the determination of trends in its further development, taking into account the on-going changes in military affairs, is *the most important task* of the theory of Soviet military art" (emphasis added, Mayorov 1985: 40). The Soviets view that wartime experience as a "rich base for reflection and its creative use in contemporary conditions" (Kozlov 1985: 17).

One clear lesson that the Soviets have drawn from their analysis of the wartime experience was expressed by Marshal Kulikov in 1975. Kulikov's analysis of strategic leadership highlights the fact that the decision making entity with responsibility for strategic direction over the armed forces, STAVKA, not in existence before the outbreak of the war and was only formed three weeks later. Although Kulikov acknowledges that this was "not a long period of time," he warns that future wars will not permit such luxuries. Kulikov concluded, "Consequently, one of the lessons of the war is that the system of strategic leadership must be thought out, elaborated, and arranged in all its details before the beginning of the war" (Kulikov 1975: 14).

One manifestation of this conclusion is the establishment of High Commands of Forces in the peripheral Theater of Strategic Military Action (TVD). Here again, the Soviets turned to their wartime experience with the establishment of intermediate commands between Moscow and the fronts. It is evident from the analyses published in various Soviet military journals that the Soviets began reconsidering their wartime experience in light of current requirements in the mid-1970s and, by 1979, they were intent on setting up some sort of intermediated command echelon in peacetime. Soviet analysis of the wartime experience emphasized the fact that operations in both the Western and Eastern theaters developed on too large a scale to permit rigid centralization to be effective based upon a STAVKA-to-front organization. The Soviets were, therefore, forced to devise alternative methods to ensure both effective control and sufficient latitude to permit the flexibility required by rapidly changing battlefield situations. As a result of these analyses, they concluded, "The experience of the world war shows that it was practically impossible for the Supreme High Command to direct the military actions of large groupings without an intermediate echelon and, as with the general system of strategic leadership, it is necessary to create it before the war, and its structure must correspond to the character and scale of the anticipated military actions" (Vyrodov 1979: 23).

Clearly, then, the Soviets are interested in the lessons to be learned from their wartime experience with strategic leadership for the fulfillment of modern decision-making requirements. They have carefully analyzed this model and appear to have concluded that much of the structure of that experience is relevant to the contemporary situation. While acknowledging the problems associated with the initial period of the war and the lack of preparation, recent treatments of the subject have focused upon the development of the Soviet Great Patriotic War strategic leadership structure after 1942 as providing the correct model for contemporary analysis. This was based on their conclusion that, in the words of Marshal Sokolov, then Minister of Defense, "From the end of 1942, the art of strategic leadership of the Soviet Armed Forces manifested itself in full measure" (cited in Gayvoronskii 1986: 21).

One objection to relying upon the wartime model could be based on the fact that the nature of war itself has changed drastically in the last 40 years. These changes have been created not just by the introduction of nuclear weapons, but also by the development of high-technology conventional weapons and modern means of intelligence collection and communications. All of this has combined to increase dramatically both the tempo of warfare and the role of time in modern combat. Marshal Ogarkov identified one major difference between contemporary war and the Great

Patriotic War as the virtual absence of "pauses" between strategic operations (Ogarkov 1982: 34–35). The Soviets seem to believe, however, that this simply increases the necessity for having a structure and process in place before the outbreak of a future war.

Notes

1 "Madrid's Diario 16 Interviews Military Leaders—Lebedev on NATO, Economy," *FBIS Daily Report* 20 August 1987.
2 Akhromeyev 1984:24. For an account of the conference see "Immortal Exploits of the People and Army." The Military Science conference devoted to the 40th anniversary of the fundamental turning point in World War II. *Krasnaya zvezda*. 24 December 1983, 2.
3 See, for example, Ogarkov 1985: 42–54. The best discussion of this in Western sources may be found in *Soviet Future War* 1987.
4 M. A. Gareyev, "Marxist-Leninist Military Science and Its Role in the Defense of the Achievements of Socialism," in Volkogonov 1984: 288.
5 See, for example, Grinkevich 1986 and the detailed analysis of these methods in Kir'yan 1986.
6 For single-front exploitation, see Kozlov 1964.
7 See the discussion in *Soviet Future War* 1987.
8 Emphasis added. Ogarkov, "Military Strategy," in *Sovetskaya Voennaya entsiklopediya*, Vol. 7, 1981: 564.
9 S. F. Akhromeyev, "The Great Victory," *Krasnaya zvezda* 9 May 1987, 2.
10 "Yazov Addresses Meetings," *FBIS Daily Report* 26 February 1988, 69.
11 "Akhromeyev on Armed Forces Anniversary, History," *FBIS Daily Report* 22 February 1988, 87.
12 See, for example, Sokolovskii 1975:28. All three versions of this work, published in 1962, 1963 and 1968, respectively, carried this reference. For a very recent reference to combat operations extending over the period of one year see Bartenev 1986: 126.
13 D. F. Ustinov, "Averting the Threat of Nuclear War," *Pravda* 1982, 4.
14 For the most recent list of such indicators, see Zashchita 1984: 173.
15 Ogarkov in *Sovetskaya Voennaya entsiklopediya*, vol. 7.
16 Kuznetsov, "Command in Transition," in Bialer 1969: 349.
17 Kuznetsov in Bialer 1969: 349.
18 V. Zemstov, "Important Factor of Victory in War," *Krasnaya zvezda* 1967: 2.
19 I. G. Zav'yalov, "Soviet Military Doctrine," *Krasnaya zvezda* March 1967.
20 V. Zemstov, "Important Factor of Victory in War," *Krasnaya zvezda* 1967: 2.
21 V. G. Kulikov, "Brain of the Army," *Pravda* 1973.

9

Conclusion

Cristann Lea Gibson

> The last war is for us not a simple fact of history. . . . For the Soviet people, war and victory are fused into one, and they will never be just history. They are our present and future. Victory in the most just of all the wars that our people ever had to wage is a subject of nationwide pride, a mighty factor in the upbringing of new generations, the creators and defenders of socialism, and a terrible warning to those who would wish once again to test our firmness.
>
> (Moscow Domestic News Service, 20 June 1986)

Over the past forty years those who have studied the Soviet Union have inevitably had to deal with the manner and extent to which the Great Patriotic War has shaped the institutions, methodology and events of the postwar world. Although in some areas of study contemporary needs may appear to overrun the vitality of the wartime experience, it still survives to teach and to remind every generation of the requirements and costs of victory. The lessons imprinted during the war have determined the very nature of the Soviet state.

Perhaps one area in which an understanding of the long-term effects of the war is crucial is in Soviet military studies. In the past, debates have raged among Western academics concerning the very history of the years 1939 to 1947, their lasting impression on Soviet structures and decision making, and the degree to which the Soviets actually believe their own historical perceptions. What they have

all agreed on is that the war occupies the central place in the postwar
development and thinking of the Soviet military. It is, therefore,
the logical starting place for any serious study of contemporary
military issues. The extent and way in which the war has effected
the modern military is therefore a key element in understanding
and analyzing the evolution of present day military affairs.

In this volume we have brought together a series of the most
important elements of contemporary Soviet military affairs and
have sought to establish their relevance to the experience of the
Great Patriotic War. We have presented the intentionally interlocking issues of historiography, risk assessment, mobilization, the
defense industry, wartime decision making and control, the
organization and structure of the General Staff, and conventional
and strategic military theory. Taken together these chapters form
a complex picture of the positive and negative influences of the war,
and at the same time they place the experience of the Great Patriotic
War in its proper, and uniquely Soviet perspective. They also put
to rest the view that the experiences of the Great Patriotic War have
been relegated to history and have little to offer the contemporary
Soviet military.

In chapter 2 Eugene Rumer has answered the real need for
creating a context of the war itself and the way in which it has been
studied by Soviety decision makers and military men, which is an
aspect of study that has been consistently overlooked. It is the
position and prominence of war history and the way in which it is
interpreted that can tell us a great deal about the most general effects
of the war experience. The extent to which the lessons of the Great
Patriotic War have become a part of generations of the professional
Soviet military is in itself a real revelation of the degree to which
the war still effects contemporary thinking. As Rumer has pointed
out, it also provides a common basis for experience and an oblique
forum for debate about sensitive subjects. Ultimately, the way
wartime history is continually rewritten to focus on issues that are
increasingly relevant in the modern world shows the importance
of linking present-day issues to the lessons of the past.

In the chapter on Soviet risk taking Jonathan Adelman has
shown that the experience of the war left the Soviets with a realistic
sense that the "costs of war and its unpredictability made peace a
necessity" and thus made them reluctant to use force in the postwar
era. The need to further secure Soviet borders by creating a security

zone—primarily in Eastern Europe and lately in Afghanistan—ultimately overrode Soviet reluctance to use force and take risks. The high-risk situations of crisis and war, however, and the Soviet preoccupation with the disastrous experience of the initial period of war, has led them to value preparedness at all costs. Finally, Adelman has shown that the image of the West—technologically formidable and duplicitous in the eyes of the Soviets—that evolved during and immediately after the war only reinforced the traditional Marxist views of capitalist states. The dominating influence of the World War II has remained, however, a real aversion to situations of high risk beyond the Soviet sphere and a desire to implement measures (arms control, troop withdrawals) that lessen the overall possibility of war.

In my chapter on mobilization I took a closer look at the costs and methods of the economic and military preparations for going to war. The experience of World War II taught the very hard lesson of the ultimate costs of being unprepared to wage a modern war. Without an expanded economic base for the defense industries prior to the war the Soviets could not have survived militarily. The war also taught the need for extended combat readiness, training and reserves of the forces, and the need for some level of autonomy with respect to territorial manning. The mobilization structure, so well tested under fire, has survived and matured but is ultimately dependent on the degree of vitality of the defense economy and the character of the initial period of war. If war begins once again as a surprise the same problems with mobilization will be virtually replicated. As the war continues on a prolonged course the structure and implementation of military mobilization based on the wartime experience will proceed much as before.

The development of the defense industry in the Soviet Union and its inheritance from the Great Patriotic War is discussed at length in Peter Almquist's pioneering chapter. From an organizational, design and production perspective Almquist draws out the specifics of the wartime and postwar defense industries. He points out the professional continuity—both in terms of personnel and experience—within design bureaus and defense industrial sectors from the war to the present day. The advanced nature of the military economy in terms of savings and efficiency has even made it the model for Gorbachev's development of the general economy in the 1990s. The lesson the war taught was the necessity for developing a strong defense industry in peacetime to eliminate the need to wait for an extensive conversion period during war.

The chapter by Dan McIntosh shows the way in which the wartime experience "has created and continues to legitimize a structure of decision making and control at the core of the Soviet systems." He examines this structure in terms of the strategic leadership and its organizational basis, and finds that its development has depended heavily on the experience of the Great Patriotic War. McIntosh also looks at the Soviet concept of control both in terms of troop control and communications and finds that the wartime experience serves as a primer on the need for timeliness and redundancy.

Finally, chapter 7 looks at the transition from peacetime to wartime command and the increased need for flexibility and speed within this process. Although the Soviets traditionally reserve this phase of command transition for the actual outbreak of hostilities, they are continually aware of the gaps in the command structure created by going to war without such a decision-making structure already in place. McIntosh finds that the wartime strategic leadership will probably function both organizationally and in terms of decision making much as it did during the previous war.

Condoleezza Rice carries the view of wartime command structures and planning to the key and often overlooked level of the General Staff and its coordination with the service and field staffs. The evolution of the organization of the General Staff and its coordination with the subordinate staffs—in terms of planning and command—that took place during the war has survived virtually intact to the present day. In addition, this centralization of control places the ultimate value on initiative and coordination of the commander and his chief of staff. Finally, the development of combined arms staffs that must centrally coordinate naval, air and ground forces is critical to ensuring the improved troop control and communications necessary to victory in war. As Rice states, "(the Soviets) understand that it is at this level, between the center, the front and the subordinate units that wars are won and lost." The war taught the Soviets that this highly developed structure of communication and coordination from the General Staff level down had to be the cornerstone of prewar planning in order to avoid the disaster of a fragmented command during the initial period of war.

In his chapter on military theory Notra Trulock takes a look at the positive and negative lessons of the war for the contemporary Soviet planner. The prewar development of military theory concerning such issues as deep operations, mobile groups, and groups of fronts is validated by the wartime experience and translates well into the postwar environment of combined nuclear and conventional operations. A more negative aspect of the war experience is the whole process of forecasting. The Great Patriotic War showed the necessity of a continuous and uninterrupted process. The failure to anticipate the nature of future war and assess correctly how war would begin could impose unaffordable costs in the initial period of war. Finally, Trulock looks at the question of strategic leadership. The widespread disruption in the initial period of the World War II virtually reduced the strategic leadership to command on an ad hoc basis. In the contemporary view there is a need to establish a strong command base prior to the outbreak of war.

Essentially this book is intended to serve as a beginning. Since Soviet analysts show an increasing interest in World War II and its relevance to modern warfare it is time for Western scholars to begin to reevaluate the wartime experience and to fill in the many gaps in our knowledge of the period. To understand the present-day military in the Soviet Union we must begin where they begin. We must be conscious of their "uses of the past" in their plans for the future.

Bibliography

Books

Adelman, Jonathan R., ed. (1986). *Superpowers and Revolution*. New York: Praeger.
——— (1988). *Prelude to the Cold War: Tsarist, Soviet and U.S. Armies in the Two World Wars*. Boulder, Colo.: Lynne Rienner Publishers.
——— (1990). *Soviet Military Intervention*. New York: Praeger.
Adomeit, Hannes (1982). *Soviet Risk Taking and Crisis Behavior*. London: Allen and Unwin.
——— (1986). *Soviet Crisis Prevention and Management: Why and When Do the Soviet Leaders Take Risk?* Rand Occasional Paper OPS-008. Santa Monica, Calif.: Rand Corporation.
Aldcroft, Derek (1978). *The European Economy 1914–1970*. New York: St. Martin's Press.
Almquist, Peter (1987). *The Organization and Influence of Soviet Military Industry, 1965–1982*. Ph.D. diss., MIT.
Altukov, P. K. (1984). *Osnovi teorii upravlenie voiskami*. Moscow: Voenizdat.
Amann, Ronald and Julian Cooper, eds. (1982). *Industrial Innovation in the Soviet Union*. New Haven, Conn.: Yale University Press.
——— (1986). *Technical Progress and Soviet Economic Development*. Oxford: Basil Blackwell.
Artiunian, Yu. (1969). *Sovet'skoe krest'yanstvo v gody velikoi otechestvennoi voiny*. Moscow: Gosizdat.

Barron, John (1974). *KGB*. New York: Reader's Digest Press.
Bartenev, S. (1986). *Ekonomicheskoe protivoborstvo v voine*. Moscow: Voenizdat.
Baxter, William P. (1986). *Soviet Airland Battle Tactics*. Novatio, Calif.: Presidio Press.
Bayer, Philip A. (1987). *The Evolution of the Soviet General Staff 1917–1941*. Ph.D. diss., University of Chicago. Reprinted in New York: Garland.

Bialer, Seweryn, ed. (1970). *Stalin and His Generals*. London: Pegasus.
——— (1980). *Stalin's Successors*. Cambridge: Cambridge University Press.
Bol'shaya Sovetskaya Entsiklopediya, 3rd ed. (1977). Vol. 27, 23–24. Moscow: Sovetskaya Entsiklopediya.
Brzezinski, Zbigniew (1961). *The Soviet Bloc*. New York: Praeger.

Carter, Ashton, John D. Steinbruner, and Charles A. Zraket, eds. (1987). *Managing Nuclear Operations*. Washington, D.C.: Brookings Institution.
Chalmeyev, V. (1978). *Malyshev*. Moscow: Molodaya Gvardiya.
Chuyev, Yu. V. and Yu. B. Mikhaylov (1975). *Forecasting in Military Affairs*. Moscow: Voenizdat. Published under the auspices of the United States Air Force. Washington, D.C.: Government Printing Office.
Clark, Alan (1965). *Barbarossa—The Russo-German Conflict 1941–1945*. New York: William Morrow.

Dawisha, Karen (1984). *The Kremlin and the Prague Spring*. Berkeley: University of California Press.
Djilas, Milovan (1962). *Conversations with Stalin*. New York: Harcourt, Brace and World.

Erickson, John (1962). *The Soviet High Command*. New York: St. Martin's Press.
——— (1975). *The Road to Stalingrad*. London: Weidenfeld.
——— (1983). *The Road to Berlin*. Boulder, Colo.: Westview Press.
Evans, Peter B., Dietrich Reuschmeyer, and Theda Skocpol, eds. (1985). *Bringing the State Back In*. Cambridge: Cambridge University Press.

Fedoseyev, P. N. (1987). *40 let velikoi pobedy*. Moscow: Nauka.
50 let vooruzhennykh sil SSSR. (1968). Moscow: Voenizdat.
Firdman, Henry (1985). *Decision-Making in the Soviet Microelectronics Industry: The Leningrad Design Bureau: A Case Study*. Falls Church, Va.: Delphic Associates.
Friedrich, Carl and Zbigniew Brzezinski (1961). *Totalitarian Dictatorship and Democracy*. New York: Praeger.

Gati, Charles (1986). *Hungary and the Soviet Bloc*. Durham, N.C.: Duke University Press.
Gareyev, M. (1985). *M. V. Frunze: voenny teoretik*. Moscow: Voenizdat.
Gibson, Cristann Lea (1983). *Patterns of Demobilization: The U.S. and U.S.S.R. After World War Two*. Ph.D. diss., University of Denver.
Golubovich, V. S. (1984). *Marshal R. Ya. Malinovskii*. Moscow: Voenizdat.

Grechko, A. A. (1975). *The Armed Forces of the Soviet State*. Moscow: Voenizdat.

Grigorenko, Petro G. (1982). *Memoirs*. New York and London: W. W. Norton.

Harrison, Mark (1985). *Soviet Planning in Peace and War 1939–1945*. Cambridge: Cambridge University Press.

Heykal, Mohammed (1978). *The Sphinx and the Commissar*. New York: Harper and Row.

Horelick, Arnold, A. Ross and John Steinbruner (1973). *The Study of Soviet Foreign Policy: A Review of Decision-Theory-Related Approaches*. R-13334. Santa Monica, Calif.: Rand Corporation.

Hyland, William G. (1987). *Mortal Rivals: Superpower Relations from Nixon to Reagan*. New York: Random House.

Istoriya velikoi otechestvennoi voiny Sovetskogo Soyuza. Vol. 1. (1960). Moscow: Voenizdat.

Istoriya vtoroi mirovoi voiny 1939–1945. Vol. 4. Moscow: Voenizdat.

Ivanov, S. P. (1966). *Nachal'ny period voiny*. Moscow: Voenizdat.

Ivanov, V. M. (1985). *Marshal M. N. Tukhachevskii*. Moscow: Voenizdat.

Jones, Ellen (1985). *Red Army and Society*. Boston: Allen and Unwin.

Jung, Hermann (1971). *Die Ardennen—Offensive 1944/45*. Frankfurt: Musterschmidt Gottingen.

Kaplan, Stephen (1981). *Diplomacy of Power—Soviet Armed Forces As a Political Instrument*. Washington, D.C.: Brookings Institution.

Kir'yan, M. M. (1982). *Voenno-tekhnicheskii progress i vooruzhennye sily*. Moscow: Voenizdat.

——— (1985). *Problemy voyennoy teorri v sovetskikh nauchno-spravochnykh izdaniyakh*. Moscow: Nauka.

——— (1986). *Vnezapnost'v nastupatel' nykh operatsiyakh velikoi otechestvennoi voiny*. Moscow: Nauka.

———, ed. (1987). *Fronty nastypali: no opyty Velikoi Otechestvennoi Voiny*. Moscow: Nauka.

Kozhevnikov, M. M. (1985). *Komand i shtab v VVS sovetskoi armii v velikoi otechestvennoi voine: 1941–1945*. Moscow: Nauka.

Kozlov, M. M. (1987). *Akademiya general'nogo shtaba*. Moscow: Voenizdat.

Kozlov, S. N. (1964). *O sovetskoi voennoi nauke*. Moscow: Voenizdat.

——— (1971). *The Officer's Handbook*. Moscow: Voenizdat. Published under the auspices of the U.S. Air Force. Washington, D.C.: Government Printing Office.

Kulich, V. M., ed. (1972). *Voennaya sila i mezhdunarodnaya otnosheniya*. Moscow: Mezhdunarodnye Otnoshenaya.

KPSS o vooruzhennykh silakh Sovetskogo Soyuza: dokumenty, 1917–1981. (1981). Moscow: Voenizdat.

KPSS: stroitel'stvo vooruzhennykh sil SSSR. (1967). Moscow: Voenizdat.

Kukushkin, Yu. S., ed. (1986). *Sovetskii tyl' v gody Velikoi Otechestvennoi Voiny*. Moscow: Vyshaya Shkola.

Kulikov, V. G., ed. (1976). *Akademiya general'nogo shtaba*. Moscow: Voenizdat.

Kuz'mina, A. (1985). *Generalnii konstruktor Pavel Sukhoi*. Minski: Belarus'.

Leebaert, Derek, ed. (1981). *Soviet Military Thinking*. Boston: Allen and Unwin.

Linz, Susan, ed. (1985). *The Impact of World War II on the Soviet Union*. Totowa, N.J.: Rowman and Allanheld.

Login, V. T. (1979). *Dialektika voenno-istoricheskogo issledovaniya*. Moscow: Nauka.

MccGwire, Michael, Ken Booth and John McConnell, eds. (1975). *Soviet Naval Policy: Objectives and Constraints*. New York: Praeger.

Mastny, Vojtech (1978). *Russia's Road to Cold War*. New York: Columbia University Press.

Medvedev, Roy (1979). *On Stalin and Stalinism*. New York: Oxford University Press.

Merimskii, V. A. (1984). *Takticheskaya podgotovka motostrelkovykh i tankovykh podrazdelenie*. Moscow: Voenizdat.

Mishin, V. P. (1985). *Osnovy proyektirovaniya letatel'nykh apparatov (transportnie sistemy)*. Moscow: Mashinostroyeniye.

Morekhina, G. G. (1986). *Partiinoe stroitel'stvoe v period Velikoi Otechestvennoi Voine Sovet'skogo Soyuza, 1941–1945*. Moscow: Politizdat.

Mylnar, Zdenek (1980). *Nightfrost in Prague*. London: Hurst.

Nekrich, A. M. (1965). *1941 22 Iyunya*. Moscow: Nauka.

Ogarkov, N. V. (1982). *Vsegda v gotovnost k zashchite otechestva*. Moscow: Voenizdat.

——— (1985). *Istoriya uchit bditel'nost*. Moscow: Voenizdat.

Platanov, V. P. and V. P. Gorbulin (1979). *Mikhailo Kuz'mich Yangel*. Kiev: Naukova Dumka.

Ploss, Sidney (1986). *Moscow and the Polish Crisis*. Boulder, Colo.: Westview Press.

Popel, N. N. (1974). *Upravleniye voiskami*. Moscow: Voenizdat.

Pospelov, P. N. (1974). *Sovet'skii tyl' v Velikoi Otechestvennoi Voiny*. Moscow: Voenizdat.

Sarkisian, S. A. and D. E. Starik (1985). *Ekonomika aviatsionnoi promyshlennosti*. Moscow: Vyshaya Shkola.

Schapiro, Leonard (1971). *The Communist Party of the Soviet Union*. 2nd ed. New York: Vintage.

Schwartz, Harry (1968). *An Introduction to the Soviet Economy*. Columbus, Ohio: Charles E. Merrill. Pub Com.

Scott, Harriet Fast and William F. Scott (1983). *The Soviet Control Structure: Capabilities for Wartime Survival*. New York: Crane Russak.

Seaton, Albert (1970). *The Russo-German War 1941–1945*. New York: Praeger.

Selected Soviet Military Writings 1970–1975. Washington, D.C.: Government Printing Office.

Shakurin, A. M. (1983). *Kryl'ya pobedy*. Moscow: Politizdat.

Shavrov, I. E. and M. I. Galkin (1977). *Metodologiya voenno-nauchnogo poznaniya*. Moscow: Voenizdat.

Shtemenko, B. M. (1981). *Generalnyi shtab v gody voiny*. Moscow: Voenizdat.

Shumikhin, V. S. (1986). *Sovetskaya voennaya aviatsiya, 1917–1941*. Moscow: Nauka.

Skirdo, M. P. (1970). *Narod, armiya, polkovodets*. Moscow: Voenizdat.

—— (1970). *The People, The Army, The Commander*, in *Soviet Military Thought*. (1970–). Moscow: Voenizdat.

Slusser, Robert (1973). *The Berlin Crisis 1961*. Baltimore: Johns Hopkins University Press.

Smith, Gerald (1985). *Doubletalk: The Story of SALT I*. Lanham, Md.: University Press of America.

Sokolovskii, V. D., ed. (1968). *Soviet Military Strategy*. Translated and edited by Harriet Fast Scott. Moscow: Voenizdat.

—— (1975). *Soviet Military Strategy*. Edited with an analysis and commentary by Harriet Fast Scott. New York: Crane, Russak & Co.

Sorokin, A. I. (1978). *Shest'desyat' let na stazhe rodiny*. Moscow: Voenizdat.

Sovetskaya voennaya entsiklopediya. (1976–80). 8 vols. Moscow: Voenizdat.

The Soviet Conduct of War. (1987). Ft. Leavenworth, Kansas: Soviet Army Studies Office.

Soviet Future War (Draft SASO Study). (1987). Ft. Leavenworth, Kansas: Soviet Army Studies Office.

Statistical Handbook of the U.S.S.R. (1965). New York: Conference Board.

Stoler, Mark (1977). *The Politics of the Second Front: American Military Planning and Diplomacy in Coalition Warfare 1941–1945*. Westport, Conn.: Greenwood Press.

Tarakanov, K. V. (1974). *Matematika i vooruzhennaya bor'ba*. Moscow: Voenizdat.

Terry, Sarah, ed. (1984). *Soviet Policy in Eastern Europe*. New Haven, Conn.: Yale University Press.

XXIII s'ezd kommunisticheskoi partii Ukrainy: materialy s'ezda. (1967). Kiev: Politizdat.

Tyushkevich, S. A. (1978). *Sovetskie vooruzhennye sil: istoriya stroitel'stva*. Moscow: Voyenizdat.

U.S. Department of Defense. *Soviet Military Power*. Annual.

Urlanis, B. (1971). *Wars and Population*. Translated by Lee Lempert. Moscow: Progress Publishers.

Valenta, Jiri (1979). *The Soviet Intervention in Czechoslovakia*. Baltimore: Johns Hopkins University Press.

Valenta, Jiri and William Potter, eds. (1984). *Soviet Decisionmaking for National Security*. London: Allen and Unwin.

Velikaya Otechestvennaya Voina Sovetskogo Soyuza, 1941–1945: Entsiklopediya. (1985). Moscow: Sovetskaya Entsiklopediya.

Velikaya Otechestvennaya Voina Sovetskogo Soyuza, 1941–1945: Kratkaya Istoriya. (1984). Moscow: Voenizdat.

Vlasov, B. V. and G. B. Kats, eds. (1985). *Organizatsiya, planirovaniye, i upravleniye predpriyatiyem massovogo mashinostroveniya*. Moscow: Vysshaya Shkola.

Voenny entsiklopedicheskii slovar'. 2 editions. (1983, 1986). Moscow: Voenizdat.

Voennye voprosy v dokumentakh KPSS i Sovetskogo gosudarstva. (1980). Moscow: Voenizdat.

Volkogonov, D. A. (1984). *Marksistsko-Leninskoye uchentiye o voine i armii*. Moscow: Voenizdat.

Vorontsov, G. F. (1976). *Voennye koalitsii i koalitsionnye voiny*. Moscow: Voenizdat.

Voznesenskii, Nikolai (1948). *The Economy of the USSR During World War II*. Translation. Washington, D.C.: Public Affairs Press.

Vtoraya mirovaya voina: itogi i uroki. (1985). Moscow: Voenizdat.

Warner, Edward L., Josephine J. Bonan, and Erma F. Packman (1987). *Key Personnel and Organizations in the Soviet Military High Command*. Rand Note N-2567-AF. Santa Monica, Calif.: Rand.

Werth, Alexander (1964). *Russia At War 1941–1945*. New York: E. P. Dutton.

Who Was Who in the USSR. (1972). Metuchen, New Jersey: Scarecrow Press.

Who's Who in the Soviet Union. (1984). Munich: K. G. Saur.

Wolfe, T. W. (1975). *Military Power and Soviet Policy*. Santa Monica, Calif.: RAND Corporation.

Wozniuk, Vladimir (1987). *From Crisis to Crisis: Soviet-Polish Relations in the 1970s*. Ames: Iowa State University Press.

Yazov, D. T. (1987). *Na strazhe sotsializma i mira*. Moscow: Voenizdat.

Zashchita ot oruzhiya massivogo porazheniya. (1984). Moscow: Voenizdat.

Zemstov, Ilya (n.d.). *Soviet Sociology*. Fairfax, Va.: Hero Books.

Zheltov, A. C. (1969). *Metodologicheskie problemy voennoi teori i praktiki*. Moscow: Voenzidat.

Zhilin, P. A. (1984). *O voine i voennoi istorii*. Moscow: Nauka.

—— (1986). *Istoriya voennogo iskusstva*. Moscow: Voenizdat.

Ziemke, Earl (1968). *Stalingrad to Berlin: The German Defeat in the East*. Washington, D.C.: Government Printing Office.

Zverev, A. G. (1946). *Gosudarstvennoi budzhei Soyuza SSSR*. Moscow: Gosfinizdat.

Articles

Akhromeyev, S. (1984). "The Role of the Soviet Union in its Armed Forces in the Achievement of the Turning Point of the Second World War and its International Significance." *Voenno-istoricheskii zhurnal'* (2).

—— (1985). "The Superiority of Soviet Military Science and Soviet Military Art—One of the Most Important Factors of Victory in the Great Patriotic War." *Kommunist* (3) (February).

Alexander, Arthur J. (1981). "Research in Soviet Defence Production." *Nato's Fifteen Nations* (October-November).

Alferov, S. (1981). "Strategicheskoye razvertivanie Sovetskikh voisk na Zapadnom TVD v 1941 godu." *Voenno-istoricheskii zhurnal'* (6).

"Allocations of Resources in the Soviet Union and China-1984." (1985). Hearing before the Subcommittee on International Trade, Finance, and Security Economics of the Joint Economic Committee. Washington, D.C.: Government Printing Office.

Babich, V. K. (1987). "Deistviya strategicheskoi aviatsii SShA v Koreye i Vietname." *Voenno-istoricheskii zhurnal'* (August).

Biery, Frederick P. (1983). "Converging Lines." *Defense & Foreign Affairs* (May).

Biryuzov, S. S. (1964). "The Lesson of the Beginning Period of the Great Patriotic War." *Voennaya mysl'* (8).

Cherednichenko, M. I. (1971). "Modern War and Economics." *Kommunist vooruzhennykh sil* (18) (September).

Cohen, Stephen (1985). "Living Memories of the Great War." *New Statesman*, 8 February.

Danilov, V. D. (1987). "Razvitiye sistemy organov strategicheskogo rukovodstva s nachalom Velikoy Otechestvennoy voyny." *Voenno-istoricheskii zhurnal'* (June).

Deane, Michael, Ilana Kass, and Andrew G. Porth (1984). "The Soviet System." *Strategic Review* 22 (3).

Editorial (1987). "Voenno-istoricheskuyu rabotu—na uroven' sovre-mennykh trebovanio." *Voenno-istoricheskii zhurnal'* (January).

Evseyev, A. I. (1985). "On Certain Trends in the Changes of the Content and Character of the Initial Period of War." *Vooruzhennye istoricheskii zhurnal'* (11).

Erickson, John (1984). "Soviet Cybermen: Men and Machines in the Soviet System." *Signal* 39 (4) (December).

FBIS Daily Report, 1987; 22, 26 February 1988.

Gavrilov, V. (1972). "Material'naya osnova ukrepleniya oboronosposob-nosti strany." *Tyl' i snabzhenie sovetskikh vooruzhyonnykh sil* (February).

Gayvoronskiy, F. F. (1986). "The Superiority of Soviet Military Science and Military Art in the Great Patriotic War," in *Vooruzhennykh istoricheskii zhurnal'* (4).

Goshcitskiyi, V. (1917, December 16). "Kakiye i dlya chego nyzhnyi stabyi." *Armiya i flot rabochei i krestyanskoi Rossii.*

Grabin, V. G. (1969). "Usovershenstvovannaya divizionnaya." *Tekhnika i vooruzheniye* (August).

Grabin, V. (1970). 'Vklad v pobedy." *Tekhnika i vooruzheniye* (May).

Grange, Judith K. (1984). "Cybernetics and Automation in Soviet Troop Control." *Signal* 39 (6).

Grinkevich, D. (1986). "The Factor of Time in Battle." *Voennyy vestnik* (11).

Hart, Douglas M. (1984). "Soviet Approaches to Crisis Management: The Military Dimension," *Survival* 26 (5) (September/October).

Herspring, Dale (1987). "On Perestroyka: Gorbachev, Yazov, and the Military." *Problems of Communism* (July/August).

Hines, John G., and Philip A. Peterson (1986). "Changing the Soviet System of Control." *International Defense Review* (3).

Ivanov, S. P. (1971). "The Initial Period of War." *Voennaya mysl'* (5).

Ivashov, L. G. (1987). "Iz opyta perevoda narodnogo khozyaistva SSSR s mirnogo na voennoye polozheniye." *Voenno-istoricheskii zhurnal'* (June).

Izvestiya 18 October 1985.

Kalerin, B. (1965). "Economic Criterion in Research on the Effectiveness of Armament." *Voennaya Mysl'* (8).

Karnozov, L. (1970). "Designer of Artillery Equipment." *Tekhnika i vooruzheniye* (January).

Kaufman, Richard (1985). "Causes of the Slowdown in Soviet Defense." *Soviet Economy* 1 (1) (January–March).

Kauk, I. (1976). "Nash opyt upravleniya kachestvom produktsii." *Tyl' i snabzheniye sovetskikh vooruzhyonnykh sil* (November).

Khorkov, A. G. (1982). "From the Experience of Ground Forces Mobilization." *Voenno-istoricheskii zhurnal'* (4) (April).

——— (1986). "Soviet Military Art." *Voenno-istoricheskii zhurnal'* (1) (January).

——— (1987). "Technicheskoye perevooruzheniye Sovetskoy armii nakaune Velikoi Otechestvennoi Voiny." *Voenno-istoricheskii zhurnal'* (6) (June).

Kohler, Gernot (1980). "The Soviet Defense Burden, 1982–1965." *Bulletin of Peace Proposals* 11 (2).

Kokoshin, A. and V. Larionov (1987). "Kurskaya bitva v svete sovremennoi oboronitel'noi doktriny." *Mirovaya ekonomika i mezhdunarodnie otnosheniya* (August).

Korniyenko, A. (1967). "Izuchat' i razvivat' teoriyu voyennoy ekonomiki." *Tekhnika i vooruzheniye* (January).

——— (1968). "The Economic Bases of the State's Military Power." *Voennaya mysl'* (8).

Kosyrev, Ye. (1971). "Razvitiye strelkobogo oruzhiya." *Tekhnika i vooruzhenie* (January).

Kotenev, A. A. (1987). "O razgrome basmacheskikh band v Sredney Azii." *Voenno-istoricheskii zhurnal'* (February).

Kozlov, M. M. (1985). "Soviet Strategic Leadership in the Years of the Great Patriotic War." *Voyenno-istoricheskiy zhurnal'* (7) (July).

Krasnaya zvezda 1967; 19 March 1974; February 1977; 3, 9 May, 23 September 1983; July 1987.

Krasner, Stephen D. (1984). "Approaches to the State: Alternative Conceptions and Historical Dynamics." *Comparative Politics* 16 (2).

Krikunov, V. P. and B. E. Pestov (1987). "Voenno-istoricheskuyu rabotu—na uroven' sovremennykh trebovaniy." *Voenno-istoricheskii zhurnal'* (September).

Kudrevatykh, Leonid. "Konstruktor V. G. Grabin." *Moskva* (6).

Kulikov, V. G. (1975). "Strategic Leadership of the Armed Forces." *Vooruzhennye istoricheskii zhurnal* (6).

——— (1975). "Stratigicheskoye rukovodstvo vooruzhenni silami." *Voenno-istoricheskii zhurnal'* (6).

Kunitskiy, P. T. (1986). "Osnovi napravleniye razvitye Sovetskikh sil v godi Velikoi Otechestvennoi Voini." *Voenno-istoricheskii zhurnal'* (2).

——— (1987). "O viborye napravleniye glavnovo udara v kampanyakh i strategicheskikh operatsiyakh." *Voenno-istoricheskii zhurnal'* (7).

Kurkotkin, S. (1984). "Converting the National Economy From Peacetime to Wartime Status During the Years of the Great Patriotic War." *Voenno-istoricheskii zhurnal'* (9) (September).

Lomov, N. (1966). "Several Problems of Control in Modern Warfare." *Voennaya mysl'* (1).

Lushev, P. G. (1987). "High Combat Readiness of the Soviet Armed Forces—An Important Factor in the Defense of Socialism." *Voenno-istoricheskii zhurnal'* (6) (June).

"Marshal Sovetskogo Soyuza, F. I. Golikov." (1980). *Voenno-istoricheskii zhurnal'* (7).

Maslyukov, Yu. D. (1978). "Vnedreniye yednoi sistemy tekhnologicheskoi podgotovki proizvodstvo." *Standarti i Kachestvo* (5) (May).

Mayorov, A. M. (1985). "Soviet Strategic Leadership in the Years of the Great Patriotic War." *Vooruzhennykh istoricheskii zhurnal'* (7).

Nikiforenko, A. (1975). "Kachestvo cherez standarty." *Tekhnika i vooruzhenie* (September).

"Oruzhiye, dostoynoye boytsa." (1977). *Voenny vestnik* (April) 25–29.

Perespyipkin, N. (1971). "Svyaz genral'nogo shtaba." *Voenno-istoricheskii zhurnal'* (6) (June).

"Period perevooruzheniya." (1974). *Tekhnika i vooruzheniye* (June).

Petrov, F. F. (1965). "Tak kovalos' oruzhiye." *Tekhnika i vooruzhenie* (October).

Pravda, 30 June 1941; 1973; 31 January, 16 March, and 13 November 1974; 1982; 29 May 1985; 3 October 1987.

"Proizvodstvo artillerskiyskogo vooruzheniya, 1941–1945." (1974). *Tekhnika i vooruzhenie* (December).

Rice, Condoleezza (1987). "The Party, the Military and Decision Authority." *World Politics* 40 (1) (October).

Sadykiewicz, Michael (1982). "Soviet Military Politics." *Survey* 26 (1).

Saksnonov, I. (1971). "Design Documentation." *Tekhnika i vooruzheniye* (August).

——— (1972). "Razrabotka konstruktorskoi dokumentatsii." *Tekhnika i vooruzhenie* (March).

Saltyikov, N. (1971). "Predstaviteli general'nogo shtaba." *Voenno-istoricheskii zhurnal'* (9) (September).

Saltykov, I. (1975). "Konstruktor i pobeda." *Standarti i kachestvo* (May).

Serebryannikov, V. (1987). "The Correlation of Political and Military Means in the Defense of Socialism." *Kommunist vooruzhennykh sil* (18) (September).

Sergeyev, Yu. (1970). "Samoye massovoye oruzhiye." *Tekhnika i vooruzhenie* (December).

Smirnov, P. (1979). "The First Five Year Plans and the Party's Military Technical Policy." *Voenno-istoricheskii zhurnal'* (4) (March).

Strode, Dan L., and Rebecca V. Strode (1983). "Diplomacy and Defense in Soviet National Defense Policy." *International Security* 8 (2) (Fall).

Taylor, John W. R. (1986). "Gallery of Soviet Aerospace Weapons." *Air Force Magazine* (March).

Tolubko, V. F. (1987). "Strategicheskoye vzaumodestiye po opity Velikoy Otechestvennoy Voyni." *Voenna-istoricheskii zhurnal'* (2).

Tsygankov, I. (1978). "Sovetskaya voennaya tekhnika: razvitiye konstruktorskoi mysli." *Tekhnika i vooruzhenie* (February).

U.S. Congress (1984a). *The Congressional Record*. August 1984.

U.S. Congress (1984b). *Allocation of Resources in the Soviet Union and China—1984, Part 10*.

U.S. Department of State (1945). OSS R and D Doc. 1004. "Russian National Income and Defense Expenditures." 8 September.

Vannikov, B. L. (1968/69). "The USSR Defense Industry on the Eve of War." (From *Notes of a People's Commissar*). *Voprosy istorii* (10) October 1968 and (1) January 1969.

Volkotrupenko, I. I. (1986). *Voenno-istoricheskii zhurnal'* (11) (November): 94.

Volkov, V. (1979). "Zapiski." *Voenno-istoricheski zhurnal'* (9).

Vyrodov, I. (1979). "On the Leadership of Military Actions of the Strategic Groupings of Forces in the Second World War." *Vooruzhennykh istoricheskii zhurnal'* (4).

Ward, Richard D. (1981). "Soviet Practice in Designing & Procuring Military Aircraft." *Astronautics and Aeronautics* (September).

Wettig, Gerhard and George G. Weickhardt (1985). "Correspondence." *Problems of Communism* 34 (3) (May/June).

Wuthnow, Robert (1985). "State Structures and Ideological Outcomes." *American Sociological Review* (50).

Yevseyev, A. I. (1985). "O nekotorikh tendenstiyakh v izmenenii soderzhanie i karaktera nachalnovo perioda voini." *Voenno-istoricheskii zhurnal'* (11).

Zakharov, M. (1971). "Kommunisticheskaya partiya i tekhnicheskoye perevooruzheniye armii i flota v gody predvoyennykh pyatiletok." *Voenno-istoricheskii zhurnal'* (February).

Zavgorodniy, N. T. (1987). "K voprosu o podgotovke slushateley i kursantov.' *Voenno-istoricheskii zhurnal'* (March).

Zav'yalov, I. G. (1967) "Soviet Military Doctrine." *Krasnaya zvezda* (March).

——— (1970). "The New Weapon and Military Art." In *Selected Soviet Military Writings 1970–1975*. Washington, D.C.: Government Printing Office.

Zemskov, V. (1969). "Wars of the Modern Era." In *Selected Readings from Military Thought 1963–1973*. Washington, D.C.: Government Printing Office.

Zhilin, P. A. (1986). Interview. *Voenno-istoricheskii zhurnal'* (November).

Zhilin, P. A. and A. L. Tinin (1986). "Study of the Problems of History." *Novaya i noveishaya istoriya* (1) (January/February).

About the Contributors

JONATHAN R. ADELMAN, editor, is Associate Professor in the Graduate School of International Studies at the University of Denver. He has been Lady Davis Visiting Associate Professor at The Hebrew University of Jerusalem in Israel and Visiting Fellow at the Institute of Contemporary International Relations in Beijing, People's Republic of China. He is the author of *The Revolutionary Armies* (1980), *Revolution, Armies and War* (1985) and *Prelude to the Cold War: Tsarist, Soviet and U.S. Armies in Two World Wars* (1988). He is the coauthor of *The Dynamics of Soviet Foreign Policy* (1988) and editor of *Communist Armies in Politics* (1982), *Terror and Communist Politics* (1984) and *Superpowers and Revolution* (1986). His articles on Soviet politics and comparative revolution have appeared in a number of journals.

CRISTANN LEA GIBSON, editor, is Research Fellow at MIT and consultant to the RAND Corporation. She is a Phi Beta Kappa graduate of the University of Denver, where she also received her Ph.D. She held a postdoctoral fellowship on the Avoiding Nuclear War project at the Kennedy School of Government at Harvard University and at the Center for International Studies at MIT.

PETER ALMQUIST is a research staff member of the Institute of Defense Analyses, Alexandria, Virginia.

DANIEL McINTOSH is a doctoral student at the Graduate School of International Studies at the University of Denver.

CONDOLEEZZA RICE is Director of Soviet and East European Affairs for the U.S. National Security Council.

EUGENE B. RUMER is a research analyst at the RAND Corporation.

NOTRA TRULOCK is Assistant Vice President for the Pacific-Sierra Research Corporation where he is an analyst of the Soviet military.

Index